An Opinionated Career

Memoirs of a Kentucky Judge

To my good friend and fellow-Rotarian,
Duane Ellis, with best regards.

John S. Palmore
11/8/03

By John S. Palmore
Former Chief Justice
Supreme Court of Kentucky

AN OPINIONATED CAREER
Memoirs of a Kentucky Judge

Library of Congress Control Number: 2003107930

The Kentucky River Press
114 Mary Bourne Drive
Georgetown, Kentucky 40324

Order on line:
www.kentuckyriverpress.com

ISBN 0-9745287-1-4

PRINTED IN THE UNITED STATES OF AMERICA.

This work is dedicated
to the memory of my friend and colleague,
the late Pleas Jones

Table of Contents

Most of the pictures shown in this work were state photographs made by Steve Mitchell.

FOREWORD

This narrative is not intended to be autobiographical in nature but is limited to the events and observations incident to the author's 23 years as an appellate judge. Whatever it lacks in organizational structure is attributable to its having been done largely in player-piano style, as it rolled out of the author's memory bank.

CHAPTER 1
ELECTION TO THE COURT OF APPEALS

1959 was an election year. Bert Combs, who had run unsuccessfully against Albert B. "Happy" Chandler for governor in 1955, was running again, this time against Happy's lieutenant governor, Harry Lee Waterfield. Although Happy had been born and raised in Henderson County and had a host of friends in the community, I had become a strong supporter of Earle Clements, and Combs was Clements' candidate. My law partner, Leonard Mitchell, and I were the only two lawyers in Henderson who had supported Combs in 1955, and we were for him again in 1959. Leonard was a native of Clay, a coal-mining town in Webster County, but had played football at Morganfield when Clements was coaching the high school team there.

For some time it appeared that Combs could not possibly win this election, because Wilson Wyatt, of Louisville, also had thrown his hat in the ring, making it a three-man race in which the two outsiders, Combs and Wyatt, would split the anti-Chandler vote and assure

Gov. Bert T. Combs
Governor of Kentucky, 1959-1963
State Photo

Waterfield's election. However, in due course Wyatt agreed to run for lieutenant governor and to run with Combs as a team, with Clements as manager of their campaign. By this time Happy had lost some of his popularity and was unable to control the election of his successor. When the news of this development arrived at our office, I'll never forget Mitchell's prancing around the corner at Main and First Streets shouting, "Ain't the candy sweet!"

At this time I had been Commonwealth's Attorney for a little over three years. Though at first I had not wanted that particular office, I had come to appreciate and enjoy it and had been successful in prosecuting some notable cases, which had not escaped the attention of Earle Clements. So, just as he had been responsible for my having the job in the first place, now he saw to it that I went to the Court of Appeals.

Palmore as Commonwealth's Attorney in Henderson, Kentucky.
December 6, 1956
Photo by Lyle G. Van Bussum

During the previous year, 1958, Judge Porter Sims, of Bowling Green, and three other members of the Court of Appeals, all of whom were of pro-Clements political persuasion, had run for re-election. Judge Sims was opposed by B. M. Vincent, of Brownsville, who had served a term in Congress and was a brother-in-law of Clifford Smith, a smart lawyer and powerful Chandler cohort. (Smith also was a Frankfort law partner of Joe Leary,

On the left is Court of Appeals Judge Porter Sims and on the right is Warren Circuit Judge John B. Rodes. Occasion was probably Judge Rodes' 80th birthday.
Ca. 1950
Photographer Unidentified

another fine lawyer and Chandler adviser.) During this campaign Judge Sims spent several days in Henderson, and I took him around the county and city and had him to dinner at our home one evening. We became great friends during that visit, and it endeared me to his step-mother and many friends in Bowling Green, as I was to learn when my own election to succeed him came up in the next year.

Judge Sims and the other three incumbent judges were re-elected, but early in the spring of 1959, shortly after the beginning of his new term, Judge Sims suffered a fatal seizure while having dinner at the Frankfort Country Club. I learned of this sad event from the *Courier-Journal* on the following morning, which was on a Saturday. The lawyers in Henderson did not open their offices on Saturday, but most of us worked behind closed doors anyway, and on this particular morning I was in my office and received a telephone call from my old friend Maxey Harlin, in Bowling Green. He told me that several of the lawyers there wanted to see Parker Duncan, who had served on the Court of Appeals with much distinction some years before but had retired because of a health problem, succeed Judge Sims, and asked if I could support Parker. I liked and respected Judge Duncan and agreed at once to support him. Incidentally, Maxey told me at the time that some of the lawyers in Bowling Green were fearful that Rodes Myers, also of Bowling Green, might run and they wanted to keep that from happening. Rodes, an eloquent orator and well-known trial lawyer, had once served a term as lieutenant governor (under Keen Johnson) and was a Chandler ally.

Within less than an hour after I had talked to Maxey my partner, Mitchell, got a call from Earle Clements asking him to find out if I would like to run for the Court of Appeals. I told Mitchell that unfortunately I had just committed myself to support Parker Duncan and could not do it. Mitchell then called Clements and reported to me that Clements' response was to the effect that "we'll work on it."

Well, a couple of weeks or so went by and I had not given another thought to the matter of running for the court. As I said, I was pretty happy with practicing law and being Commonwealth's Attorney anyway. Meanwhile, Parker Duncan had filed, Happy had appointed Tom Sandidge, of Owensboro, to fill the vacancy until the next election, and my fellow-townsman Bill Sullivan had announced his candidacy. So the race was going to be between Bill and Parker Duncan. Bill, incidentally, had been serving as Commissioner of Aeronautics in the Chandler administration, and at the beginning of his career had been a law clerk for the Court of Appeals. His father-in-law, John Dorsey, one of the ablest lawyers I ever knew, had known Happy Chandler as a boy, and all of his people were stout Chandler supporters. But anyway, on a Sunday night after I had gone to sleep the telephone rang and it was Earle Clements, calling from the Combs-Wyatt headquarters at the Seelbach Hotel in Louisville. The first thing he said was, "Well, are you ready to run?" To say the least, I was flabbergasted. And embarrassed. Bill's friends were already circulating a petition for all of the lawyers in town to sign, supporting his candidacy, and in view of the fact that I had previously pledged my support to Parker Duncan, Mitchell and I were trying to stay out of sight. Clements said, however, that Combs and Wyatt were having a big rally at the Seelbach Hotel in Louisville on the next Tuesday night and that Parker was going to withdraw in my favor and introduce me to the crowd. He gave me Combs' room number and told me to call Combs and tell him I would run, and that if it was not okay with Combs, to call him back. So I called Bert, and he was very cordial and agreeable to my running. Incidentally, Combs and Duncan had served together on the court, and there may have been some reluctance on Bert's part to replacing Parker as the Clements candidate, though in the long years of friendship between Combs and me afterward Combs insisted that it really had been his idea. Anyhow, I agreed to do it, and it was done just as Clements said it would be.

Immediately following the speeches Clements had me go to a big room in the hotel where he had Doc Beauchamp and all or most of the Democratic chairmen from my 16-county district gathered to meet me and sign nomination papers which had been prepared in advance by Scotty Hamilton, the Commonwealth's Attorney for Jefferson County. While all this was going on we listened to a radio news broadcast which included an account of the events that had just taken place at the political rally, and when the surprise switch from Duncan to me was reported, Bill Sullivan was quoted as saying that he was out on a limb and "they were trying to cut it off." At this point Clements and Beauchamp jumped up and danced around the room in high glee. Both of them at that time were quite portly, and it gave the appearance of two elephants doing a comic ballet skit. And amid all the laughter and shouting Clements delivered this punch line that I'll never forget: "Now, by God, the fuckors have become the fuckees!" This little incident is a good illustration of the animosity between the Clements and Chandler factions of the Democratic party at the flood tide of their rivalry.

Right after these events, before we left the hotel, Earle drew me aside and gave me some sage advice on how to conduct my campaign. First, he said, get on the telephone right now, call your cousin Dr. Palmore, and tell him you are running – don't let him have to learn it from the newspapers. He is for Waterfield, but he can help you in Warren County. Dr. Cecil Palmore, who was practicing medicine in Horse Cave with his father, my Uncle Ellsworth, when I was a boy, had bought a beautiful place near Bowling Green and had served a term in the state legislature from that community. While in Frankfort I think he and Harry Lee Waterfield roomed at the old Southern Hotel on Second Street, and they had become good friends. Needless to say, I followed this sound advice from a political master, and everything went well. Cecil accepted my candidacy with the very best of good grace, and spoke in my behalf to all of his friends with whom he felt that he had influence. When I went to see him several days after calling him from the Seelbach, he told me that Bill also had contacted him and asked for his help, but he had told Bill that politics to the contrary, "this is family."

At a meeting of some kind in Louisville just after I had filed my nomination papers I ran into Paul Carter, of Tompkinsville, in the elevator at the old Kentucky Hotel. A cousin of the renowned Circuit Judge James C. Carter, titular head of the powerful Carter family in that neck of the woods, Paul was the Commonwealth's Attorney, and I had come to know him through the Commonwealth's Attorneys' Association. When Paul saw me he asked whether I had filed for the Republican nomination as well as the Democratic, and I told him that I had. He immediately pulled out of his coat pocket a petition for his own nomination on the Republican ticket and said that since I was running he would not file it. The district was heavily Democratic, and there was little or no chance that he could have won in the fall election anyway, but that was a heart-warming gesture that I will never forget, and I loved Paul Carter until the day he died.

Another memorable event during this campaign occurred when I visited Tompkinsville for the first time. My father having been born and raised in that heavily-Republican county, he and his family were well known to the Carters. My dad was a noted pistol shot and had been a member of the United States pistol team in 1924. Most of the face-card figures in Monroe County knew who he was, and even though I had done the awful thing of becoming a Democrat, the Carter family welcomed me with open arms. In 1959 no one in this century had occupied the office of circuit judge in that district except for Jim Carter and his father, James C. Carter, Sr. The day I got there in the spring of 1959 court was in session, and when I walked into the courtroom Judge Carter stopped the court proceedings and gave me a rousing introduction to the people in the courtroom. I think that was the first time I had ever met this remarkable man, and in the years thereafter and until his death we were warm friends. I also came to know and revere his great brother Dr. Tim Lee Carter, who in later times served for many years as a member of Congress.

The race between Bill and me was, of course, very largely affected by the Chandler-Clements schism within the party. As I have said, Happy had lost much of his once-fabulous popularity, and the Combs-Wyatt team won the second appellate court district and the rest of the state in general. At that time a candidate for judicial office was permitted to run in both the Democratic and Republican primaries, which both Bill and I did. Thanks to the great help of Earle Clements and Doc Beauchamp, and of J. R. Miller in Owensboro, I was fortunate to carry all 16 counties in the Republican primary and 14 of the 16 in the Democratic primary. Our campaign was pretty civil and, as had been the case when I ran against Carl Melton in the 1956 Commonwealth's Attorney race, my opponent was a gentleman and an honorable man. In that day and age the public in our part of the world would not have tolerated the type of campaign that is in vogue today.

Bill and I have been good friends through the years since that time, and I have great respect and admiration for him – as I did for Mr. Dorsey.

Having won both the Democratic and Republican primaries, I did not have any opposition in the fall election. During the interim I continued with my duties as Commonwealth's Attorney and practiced several civil cases in Henderson, Union, and Webster Counties. Shortly after the November election, however, a strange development took place. Clements and Beauchamp wanted me to hold off being sworn in as a member of the court until after Combs' inauguration (on the fifth Tuesday following the election) so that he rather than Chandler could make the temporary appointment of my successor as Commonwealth's Attorney. Judge Morris Montgomery, on the other hand, Chief Justice of the court, insisted that

The formal swearing-in ceremony in the courtroom of the Court of Appeals inside the Kentucky State Capitol.
November 20, 1959
State Photo

Judge Palmore and wife, Eleanor
November 20, 1959
State Photo

I take the oath of office and join the court promptly, because the court was overloaded with work and was far behind with its docket. (I marvel at this today, as I look back on it, because Morris was very much of a politician and a stout Clements man, and it seems remarkable that apparently there had been no discussion of the matter between them.) I was willing to cooperate in this respect until I was warned by Bob Posey, former Mayor of Henderson, that he had it on good authority that if I did not take the office right away Chandler was going to declare it vacant and appoint another judge anyway. Though I did not believe that such an appointment would be valid, certainly it would have precipitated a lawsuit that I felt would be embarrassing to the court as well as to myself. Meanwhile, to make sure that I would not be able to assume the office prematurely (!), through the exercise of his magical powers Doc Beauchamp saw to it that the Election Commission held up the issuance of my election certificate. I was really in a sweat, but at last I went ahead and was sworn in by the court on November 20, 1959, without a certificate of election. Meanwhile, however, to guard against any attempt by the governor to declare that my failure to take office had resulted in a vacancy, I secretly had my secretary, Jane Bach, who was a notary public, administer the constitutional oath of office to me at our office in Henderson.

Judge Palmore, Doc Beauchamp, and Clay Wade Bailey.
October 25, 1961
Going Away Party for Wendell Ford

An irate Doc Beauchamp erupted immediately and gave me unshirted hell over the telephone, and for the first time I

The Kentucky Court of Appeals as it appeared at the end of 1959. From the left are Palmore, Brady Stewart, Robert Bird, Morris Montgomery, James Milliken, John Moremen, and Squire Williams.

1959

State Photo

Cammack, of Frankfort, Morris Montgomery, of Liberty, and Robert Bird, of London. The Chief Justiceship was rotated, by agreement, so that each judge would hold the title for a year or a year and a half at some time during his eight-year term. Judge Cammack, who had been succeeded as Chief Justice by Judge Montgomery, died in New York during the summer of 1958 while attending the Appellate Judge's Seminar. Amos Eblen was appointed to take his place as a member of the court until the 1959 election, and as I have said, after the death of Judge Sims early in 1959 Tom Sandidge also was appointed to serve until the next election. Both of these appointed judges, incidentally, were top-flight lawyers.

All of the judges were Democrats except for Bob Bird, a Republican. Brady Stewart had been County Judge of McCracken County and was a loyal friend of Earle Clements. John Moremen had been the Director of Public Safety in Louisville (he said the greatest

The first meeting of the governor and the appellate court judges. From the left, Squire Williams, Beverly Waddill, James Milliken, Robert Cullen, Brady Stewart, Robert Bird, Morris Montgomery, Gov. Bert Combs, John Moremen, Watson Clay, Palmore, Osso Stanley, and Lt. Gov. Wilson Wyatt.
Ca. 1959-60
State Photo

thing about that job was that whenever there was a big fire he got to ride to it and wear a fireman's hat). Amos Eblen was a former law professor at U.K. and at the time of his appointment was practicing law in Lexington. Jim Milliken had been a state senator when he ran successfully for the court upon the retirement of Judge William Rees, an outstanding jurist from Maysville. Tom Sandidge was an excellent lawyer who had practiced for many years in Owensboro. Morris Montgomery had been a state senator, following in the footsteps of his father, Senator Charlie Montgomery. When he came onto the court he moved to Lawrenceburg, the home town of his wife, Frances ("Tansy"). Bob Bird, a native of Mt. Vernon, had practiced in London, and at some point had worked for the state in the wake of alcoholic problems that evidently dampened his career as a lawyer. He was elected to the court over the incumbent, Astor Hogg, in the Eisenhower landslide of 1956, the same election that took Earle Clements out of the U.S. Senate in favor of Thruston Morton. Having mentioned Bob's alcoholic problem, let me hasten to say in his defense that he had a clear, incisive mind and an excellent knowledge of law. Usually his opinions, though not frequent, were short, accurate, and to the point. I liked the man very much (despite his being an unreconstructed, hard-boiled Republican). Squire Williams, who succeeded Judge Eblen, was a native of Frenchburg, in Menifee County, and was practicing law in Frankfort at the time he ran for the court in 1959. Politically, he and I, along with Brady Stewart, John Moremen, and Montgomery, were essentially from the Clements side of the Democratic party. Milliken also had sided with the others in the 1958 controversy between Chandler and the court over who had the right to appoint the Clerk of the court following the death of the beloved Charlie O'Connell.

In addition to the seven judges we had four commissioners. Many years before, as the court became overloaded with cases and behind in its work, the legislature had authorized it to appoint commissioners to assist in considering and deciding cases. For a more detailed history the reader is referred to my article "The Commissioners of the Kentucky Court of Appeals, 1906-1976" in the Winter 1991 issue of the *Kentucky Bench and Bar* (Vol. 55, p. 12). They were required to have the same legal qualifications as the judges, and they wrote opinions for the court, but of course could not vote on any decision. In 1959 the four commissioners were Osso Stanley, Beverly Waddill, Robert Cullen and Watson Clay. All of them were exceptional lawyers and good writers. They participated in all the conferences and handled cases in exactly the same way as the judges. The court was infinitely stronger than it would have been without them. With their constant attention and help, it was not easy for the court to go very far wrong.

B. The Salary Case – A Rough Beginning

At the time of my election in 1959 the Court of Appeals had before it the case of *Board of Education of Graves County v. De Weese*, involving the constitutionality of a statute declaring that all officers and employees of school districts were to be deemed officers and employees of the state, and thus not subject to the $7,200 per annum limit imposed on local officers by Section 246 of the Constitution. Also involved was the question of whether by increasing the superintendent's compensation the school board had violated Sections 161 and 235 of the Constitution, which prohibit changing the compensation of an officer during his term of office. The circuit court had determined that there was no constitutional violation, but in a 4 to 3 decision the Court of Appeals held otherwise, and a petition for rehearing had been filed. This was the posture of the matter in the summer of 1959.

One of the judges in the majority was Tom Sandidge, and one of the dissenting judges was Amos Eblen.

Before 1949, Section 246 of the Kentucky Constitution limited the compensation of all officers of the state or any of its agencies or subdivisions to $5,000 per annum, and Section 235 prohibited any change in the compensation of a public officer during his term of office. Section 161 prohibited changing the compensation of any city, county or other municipal officer after his appointment or election or during his term of office. In 1948 the legislature proposed an amendment to Section 246 fixing the maximum compensation of the mayor of a first-class city, members of the then Court of Appeals, and all public officers with statewide jurisdiction at $12,000, circuit judges $8,400, and all other public officers $7,200. By a narrow vote, this amendment was passed in the November election of 1949.

Strangely, the amendment began by directing that no public "officer *or employee"* (italics added) other than the governor shall receive compensation in excess of the amounts set forth below, but in naming the specific categories of public servants covered by the amendment, never repeated the word "employee." Specifically, for example, the $12,000 and $7,200 limits applied to "public officers." So, perceiving the amendment as drawn by the legislature to be ambiguous, the Attorney General concluded that the words "or employee" were meaningless, and omitted them from the question as submitted to a vote of the people. In a suit brought prior to the election the Court of Appeals, in a unanimous opinion, agreed with the Attorney General. Hence Section 246 as amended in 1949 did not (and does not today) apply to "employees" *vis-à-vis* "officers," for the simple shoelaces enough, the public would loosen them up by a constitutional amendment. I recall, for example, an instance in which I chanced to witness a friendly argument on the subject between Judge Eblen and Judge Sandidge in Judge Eblen's office, one day in the summer of 1959, before I became a member of the court. Tom was saying just what I have mentioned, that if the court held fast to the decision as it stood, the people would be forced to amend the Constitution, as they had done in 1949. Amos replied, with some vigor, that no such thing would happen, and said something to the effect that, "Tom, you know they counted that thing in anyway" (referring to the 1949 amendment). That was my first introduction to the scuttlebutt that in the 1949 election Governor Earle Clements had the vote-count on the amendment held up in one or more eastern Kentucky counties until they could see how many votes were needed to pass it. (I have heard since that this happened in Pendleton County, but it is mere hearsay, and I am not sure I heard it from anyone who purported to know it was true.)

Anyway, to get back to the main stream of this story, the proposed call for a convention was defeated in the November 1960 election, and our new opinion holding that the constitutional salary limitations apply only to officers specifically named in the instrument itself was handed down on December 16, the following month.

The announcement of this new opinion, with its unorthodox history and a sharply divided court, hit with a great splash, and those of us who were responsible for it were denounced and vilified on one hand and toasted on the other. My uncle, H. D. Palmore, an engineer and prominent alumnus of the University of Kentucky, good-naturedly told me that the people over at U.K. were about ready to elect me president of the U.S. Happy Chandler, on the other hand, said that the court had cynically waited to issue its new decision until it saw whether the convention call was going to pass. Certainly it looked that way, and I can't blame him for thinking so, but in fact it was not true. I had tried all summer and fall to get the opinion out, but it just wasn't possible until three other judges were satisfied with it, and until the judges who did not like it had been allowed sufficient time to write their dissenting opinions and circulate them around to the rest of the court.

So that is the story of the salary case. The final opinion appears in 343 S.W.2d 598 (1960). Though it may have upset some of the earlier decisions and philosophies of the court, it did no violence to the text of Section 246 as it had been summarized on the ballot in the 1949 election.

C. The Bonus and Frankfort Mayor Cases

Another hot case on the griddle when I came onto the court was the Frankfort Mayor case, the issue being whether the term of Mayor John Gerard, who had been elected in 1957, was four years or, by reason of Frankfort's having changed from a third-class to a second-class city, was cut off at the end of two years. Judge W. B. Ardery, the trial judge, had decided against Mayor Gerard, and without Squire Williams and myself, neither of whom had heard the arguments of counsel or had participated in the conferences in which a tentative decision had been reached, the vote on our court stood 3 to 2 for affirming. Squire and I both agreed with the majority, but neither of us wanted to sit (that is, to take part in the decision). Had both of us recused, under the Constitution it would have been necessary for the governor to appoint two special judges, which of course would necessarily have resulted in a considerable delay in settling a controversy that needed to be resolved as soon as possible. For Squire the problem was much more acute than it was for me. It involved his town and his friends. Ben Fowler, who was counsel for Mr. Gerard, was one of his closest friends. Whichever way he voted, if he had to vote, it would cause him a good deal of embarrassment and hard feelings. To me it did not make

Squire N. Williams, Jr.
1959
State Photo

that much difference, so I agreed to take him off the hook. The result would have been the same either way, but this way avoided unnecessary damage to Squire. I took some slings and slurs around town and a nasty letter or two (unsigned, of course), and probably John Gerard never forgave me, but that is how the chips fell.

The Frankfort case was a local affair. The bonus case was really a big one. Fortunately, in this instance there was no special involvement on my part. At its 1958 regular session the legislature had proposed a constitutional amendment providing for the financing of a military veterans' bonus. Its popularity was seized upon as an aid to the candidacy of Bert Combs through the slogan, "Bert and the Bonus!" and it was approved by the public at the November 1959 general election. Shortly thereafter a suit was filed in the Franklin Circuit Court challenging its validity. The trial court (again Judge Ardery) held that the legislative action violated Section 57 of the Constitution, which provides that a member of the legislature may not vote on any measure in which he has a personal interest, because several of the legislators were veterans who would benefit from the contemplated bonus.

In an opinion written by Commissioner Watson Clay our court reversed the judgment and upheld the action of the people – not as a constitutional amendment, but as a referendum authorized by Section 50 of the Constitution. Though it was not invalid on the ground suggested by the trial court, there were other deficiencies that did make it ineffective as a constitutional amendment. I have always thought that this ingenious opinion by Judge Clay was a brilliant example of jurisprudence, because it gave effect to the will and intention of the people on a perfectly logical theory that had never been mentioned or

Watson Clay
Ca. 1970
Courtesy of Sally Clay Lanham

argued by the lawyers in the case – and had not originated in the mind of any of the judges. In simple terms, the so-called amendment was upheld on the basis of what it really was instead of what it was called. This opinion is a perfect illustration of the point I have already mentioned, that the commissioners of the court gave it a great deal of intellectual strength it would not have had without them (and never has had since the office was eventually discontinued). Originally issued on January 19, 1960, the opinion appears at 332 S.W.2d 256.

Another case of constitutional importance in the 1960's was *American Beauty Homes Corp. v. Louisville and Jefferson County Planning and Zoning Commission*, Ky., 379 S.W.2d 450 (1964), which again brought forth an absolute gem of an opinion from the pen of Watson Clay. It invalidated a statute giving the circuit court the power to decide *de novo* a zoning application coming before it on appeal from a decision of the county planning and zoning commission. If this opinion on the constitutional separation of powers is not required reading for all students in our law schools, it should be.

D. The New York Appellate Judges' Seminar

In the summer of each year 20 or so new appellate judges are invited to participate in an appellate judges' seminar at New York University Law School in New York. It runs for ten days or so, and the participants are housed in an apartment building on Washington Square normally occupied during the winter by members of the law school faculty. The members of the seminar faculty are outstanding judges and scholars from all over the country. I had the good fortune of attending this seminar in 1961. It was conducted by Dean Robert Leflar, of the University of Arkansas Law School, and among the faculty and attendees were U.S. Supreme Court Justice Bill Brennan, U.S. Circuit Court of Appeals Judges Harry Blackmun (later elevated to the U.S. Supreme Court), Fred Hamley, Simon Sobeloff, and Sterry Waterman, several notable state supreme court justices such as the great Roger Traynor of California and Wally Schaeffer of Illinois, the Chief Justice of Canada, and legal scholars like Karl Llewellyn. This was an extremely collegial group of people, and we had ample

Participants in the New York Appellate Judge's Seminar, seated from the left, Ott, Hamilton, Proctor, Sobeloff, Waterman, Cartwright, Berry, Sanders, Kelly, Jackson, Snell, Hamley, Grice. Standing from the left, Leflar, Green, Elliott, William Brennan, Schaefer, Kenison, Karl Llewellyn, Warren Burger, Harry Blackmun, Simpson, Arend, Palmore, Frantz, Broadfoot, McFadden, Knutson, Udall, Chavez, Traynor, Smith, Souris, Hattie Klein, Spencer, and Desmond.
July 24, 1961
New York University Photo

opportunity to get acquainted with each other, usually over a beer or two at a local watering hole in the late afternoon before dinner. In later years, though I did not always see eye to eye with his more liberal opinions, I never lost my admiration for Justice Brennan, who was always friendly and accessible and willing to discuss judicial philosophy. It is no wonder that he had such great influence with the other members of the Supreme Court. Right or wrong, I believe he had more to do with what the U.S. Constitution has come to mean today than any other judge in its history. [See my article, "The Bill of Rights," at page 16 of the Summer 1992 *Kentucky Bench and Bar* (Vol. 56, No. 3).]

I made some wonderful friends at the New York Seminar. Ted Souris, then a young judge on the Michigan Supreme Court, remained one of my best friends until his death in 2002. I think that he and I were the youngest members of the group. Most of the others are now gone. The most colorful of them all was Robert T. Simpson, of the Alabama Supreme Court, who had recently married and was still honeymooning with his sprightly wife, Sally. She called him "Big Judge," and he called her "Little Sally." They had been married by Judge Simpson's old friend Justice Hugo Black, of the U.S. Supreme Court. In those days, of course, the South was still the Old South, and I can still hear Big Judge wheedling Justice Brennan to be a little less liberal in his viewpoints. Sadly, not many years later Little Sally was killed in an automobile collision which happened while she and Big Judge were driving in Montgomery, Alabama, and he died not too many years afterward.

E. The "Rubber Dollar" Decision and Other Notable Cases of the 1960's

The liberating effect of our decision in the 1960 salary case did not suffice to hold the horses for very long. Along came *Matthews v. Allen*, Ky., 360 S.W.2d 135 (1962), the "rubber dollar" case, in which the 1962 legislature had raised the annual salaries of circuit judges from $8,400 (the limit set by Section 246 of the Constitution) to $10,800 through the device of making them special commissioners of the Court of Appeals. In an opinion by Judge Milliken the court upheld this action, but took the further step of declaring that the dollar limits specified in Sections 235 and 246 may be applied in terms of the current purchasing power of the 1949 dollar. From a practical standpoint this left the salary limits in shreds.

For some unaccountable reason I have no recollection of hearing the rubber dollar theory discussed or passed on in the court conference or conferences. I certainly favored affirming the validity of the legislation because I had long since, in preliminarily drafting the *DeWeese* opinion, accepted the idea that the legislature could properly confer statewide status upon certain offices or positions. And I do not now question the rubber dollar theory. In fact, it seems to me that it has worked quite well, for which I think Judge Milliken deserves great credit, because not only did he write the opinion, but I know it was his own idea to start with. He spent many a waking hour dreaming about how the compensation of the judiciary could be elevated, and he was responsible for the eventual adoption of a judicial retirement system.

In those days it was easy for a judge to modify or amplify one of his opinions after it had been finally approved in conference (and it still may be, though I do not know) and before it was sent to the clerk's office along with the record of the case. Ordinarily such changes were minor in nature, and I don't believe it happened in the rubber dollar case, but I used to wonder about it. In any event, it was a great opinion.

Of all the decisions handed down by the court during my 23 years as a member I think that the biggest block-buster, at least publicity-wise, was the 100 percent tax assessment case, *Russman v. Luckett,* Ky., 391 S.W.2d 694, decided on June 8, 1965. Section 172 of the Kentucky Constitution had always required that all taxable property be assessed at "its fair cash value," but it had never been enforced or complied with. The median rate at which real estate was being assessed throughout the state was 27 percent rather than 100 percent. Section 157 of the Constitution limits the rate at which the various cities, counties and other taxing authorities of the state, such as school districts, may tax property to so much per $100 of the value of the property to be taxed. For example, the maximum rate for counties and school districts is 50 cents per $100. If the fair value of a piece of real estate is $10,000, the maximum school tax is $50, but if it is assessed at $2,700 instead of its actual value of $10,000 the maximum tax is $13.50. In a district where property was being assessed at 12½ percent of its actual value the maximum tax was $6.25. The result of this situation was, of course, that the amount of money that could be raised by any taxing authority in the state was fixed not by the Constitution, but by its tax assessor. In counties, this was an elected officer.

In earlier cases the courts had managed to evade any head-on confrontation of this issue. But the schools, in particular, suffered more every day from the inability of their governing officials to raise the funds the Constitution (and implementing statutes) entitled them to raise. In a suit challenging the continued existence of this iniquitous situation the court finally ended it.

At that time all cases that came to the court were assigned by the Chief Justice to the various judges and commissioners. Most such assignments were perfunctory and routine. Usually the Chief would look at the records just long enough to see that no judge received a case from his own district – unless, of course, there was some special urgency about the matter as, for example, in the instance of an election question. Anyway, this case went to Watson Clay, and I had never even heard of it until he brought it into conference to be discussed and decided. I have a rather vivid recollection of that occasion for the simple reason that we all fully realized we were dealing with political dynamite. When Watson finished stating the case he said that in his opinion there was only one correct and honest answer, and that was to enforce what the Constitution commanded. To my surprise, seven hands were raised as one, without argument, without question, and without further comment. I regard this as the Court's finest moment during the entire time I was privileged to be one of its members. And again, my hat is off to Watson Clay, who handled the case and wrote the opinion.

At first blush Governor Breathitt expressed delight at this decision which offered so much hope for the financially beleaguered schools, but thanks to misleading headlines in some of the widely read newspapers of the state a great many people reacted strongly and loudly against it. Some people, for example, appeared to believe that 100 percent assessments meant 100 percent tax rates. The governor ducked, and called a special session of the legislature to rectify the apparent disaster. The result was the famous (or infamous) House Bill 1, which in substance provided that no county could raise revenue from ad valorem taxes above the amount raised in the previous year, plus 10 percent. In other words, in lieu of the 50-cent limit prescribed by Section 172 of the Constitution, the new legislatively-enacted limit was whatever amount the county had raised in the previous year, plus 10 percent. Whereas the limit prescribed by the Constitution was a uniform 50 cents per $100 for every county, under House Bill 1 every county now had a different limit, based upon what it had done before.

In due course House Bill 1 was challenged on constitutional grounds but was upheld by our court in *Rea v. Gallatin County Fiscal Court,* Ky., 422 S.W.2d 134 (1967). Meanwhile, two of our judges who had taken part in the *Russman* case had been defeated for reelection, and in each of their contests their participation in that case had been used against them. I do not know, of course, if that issue caused their defeat, but when the court voted on the *Gallatin County* case the notable courage the judges had shown in the *Russman* case had faded away. Frankly, I thought that House Bill 1 did not comport with the Constitution, but some of my friends persuaded me not to say so in the form of a dissenting opinion, so I merely had my name omitted from the enumeration of the judges who concurred in the official opinion. As I write this I am sorry to say that in substance this nefarious piece of legislation is still alive. Incidentally, I had been reelected in 1966 without opposition.

Another important case that came up during the '60's was *Kupper v. Fiscal Court of Jefferson County,* Ky., 346 S.W.2d 766 (1961), involving the constitutional validity of a 1960 legislative act (codified as KRS 68.190) applicable only to Jefferson County, authorizing the county to levy an occupational license tax. Unfortunately, this one was assigned to me, and after a considerable amount of study I concluded that the act was invalid because in effect it exempted those who had paid a similar tax to the City of Louisville. Some of the other members of the court did not like it, but they approved my opinion anyway, and it was handed down as a unanimous decision. It was not long before it began to thunder. One day I came across Charlie Farnsley (former Mayor of Louisville) huddling with John Moremen in John's office. Then I ran across Lawrence Wetherby out in the hallway on the second floor of the Capitol looking for Squire Williams. A day or so afterward John told me that we were going to have to take my opinion back. There was by this time, of course, a petition for rehearing, and when it came up in conference you can guess the answer. My opinion became a dissenting opinion, in which only Bob Bird, the solitary Republican on the Court, concurred.

I do not intend here to cast any criticism or aspersions on my fellow judges at the time. The case was of great importance to Jefferson County, and it was inevitable that lots of heat would be put on in the right places by the right people. From a pragmatic standpoint the final decision probably was in accordance with common sense. I still feel, however, as I said in my dissenting opinion, that it is fundamentally unfair that some of the people who work in Jefferson County, solely because they do their work in Louisville and pay a similar tax to the city, be excused from paying a tax that all others who work in the county must pay. After all, work done in Louisville also is work done in Jefferson County. Nobody would suggest that those who pay city property taxes should be allowed to deduct them from their state and county property taxes. One thing is sure – I was on the wrong political side of this particular case.

F. More Cases of Legal Significance in the '60's

All of the cases discussed thus far have been those in which there was an unusual public interest. There were many others, of course, that were of interest mainly to the legal profession, and in this section my purpose is to discuss those that I remember as having to some degree contributed to the growth or evolution of the law. And of course the ones I remember best are the ones in which I wrote the opinions for the court. This is not a matter of ego – it is just that I do not have the time or inclination to dig through a generation of the reports and produce a textbook.

During the '60's we had a great many land condemnation cases arising out of highway construction, and this occasioned a number of developments in the law of eminent domain. For example, in a partial taking case the traditional formula for assessing the landowner's damage was to add the market value of the portion taken to the resulting "damage to the remainder." This was changed in *Department of Highways* v. *Sherrod,* Ky., 367 S.W.2d 844 (1963), to the simple and more direct method of awarding the landowner the difference between the value of his property before the taking and the value of what he had left afterward. That opinion, written by Commissioner Robert Cullen, one of the finest scholars ever to sit with the court, is a leading case today. The decisions of our court in this field drew a good deal of interest from outside the state, as a result of which I was invited in 1967 to deliver an address on the subject of damages recoverable in a partial taking at S.M.U. in Dallas. (Published in Vol. 21, page 740, *Southwestern Law Journal.*) In these cases – especially the ones from eastern Kentucky arising in connection with

Mountain Parkway – we leaned over backward to uphold the awards made by the local juries even though we all thought they were pretty liberal. I seem to recall one instance, for example, when we reversed an award as excessive and then upon a retrial of the case another jury gave the owner even more. We always had to hassle with Morris Montgomery in these cases, because he was the least liberal member of the court on the subject of money damages regardless of the type of case, whether condemnation or personal injury. He was a fine, congenial person, well liked by everybody in our judicial family, but he probably wrote more dissenting opinions than anyone else during his time on the court. He and his vivacious wife "Tansy" were killed in a tragic automobile accident in Illinois while returning from the Conference of Chief Justices held at Colorado Springs in the summer of 1969.

Some of the other decisions that broke new ground in the '60's were:

Terry v. Associated Stone Co., Ky., 334 S.W.2d 926 (1960), a workers' compensation case holding that a disabling heart attack resulting from pre-existing disease but triggered by the claimant's work is compensable.

Turnpike Authority of Kentucky v. Wall, Ky., 336 S.W.2d 551 (1960), approving the financing of toll turnpikes through revenue bonds payable in part from future gasoline taxes reasonably identified as derived from vehicular use of the particular turnpike being financed. The opinion also upheld a provision that the lease from the Turnpike Authority to the highway department would be automatically renewed for each future biennium in the absence of affirmative action by the legislature to terminate it, thus avoiding unconstitutionality as a commitment reaching beyond the current biennium.

Blue Diamond Coal Company v. Neace, Ky., 337 S.W.2d 725 (1960), holding that under a deed giving the mineral owner the right to use the surface in "any manner that may be deemed necessary and convenient" in mining the coal the mineral owner had the right to auger mine. This was my first acquaintance with the "broad form" deed, and I was pretty well influenced by the advice of Monty Montgomery, who as Chief Justice assigned the case to me and had written the opinion in

Buchanan v. Watson, Ky., 290 S.W.2d 40 (1956), which was to become the bellwether case on the subject and the *bete noir* of the forces that eventually overthrew the broad form deed through the passage of a constitutional amendment some years after my departure from the court. That fight will be the subject of a subsequent chapter in this saga.

Louisville Refining Company v. Mudd, Ky., 339 S.W.2d 181 (1960), adopting a new approach in determining the existence of a private nuisance. This opinion became an important source in the drafting and enactment of Kentucky's 1991 Nuisance Act, which codified the existing law on the subject and is fully discussed in an article entitled "Kentucky's New Nuisance Statute," which I later wrote for the *Journal of Mineral Law and Policy,* 7 ML&P 1 (1991-92).

Lincoln Bank & Trust Company v. Queenan, Ky., 344 S.W.2d 383 (1960), construing the Uniform Commercial Code (KRS Chapter 355) which had been recently enacted by the legislature. Looking back over the years I am moved to say that not many cases have been produced, examined and practiced by such an array of fine lawyers – all of whom, regrettably, have long since departed this life. The drafting of the work was done under the hand of Dee Akers, the litigation was handled by Robert Hatton and Jack Fulton for one side and by Charlie Dobbins and Jim Thornberry for the other, and the trial proceeding was conducted by the greatest chancellor I have had the privilege of knowing, Stuart Lampe. Each of these men was a superb lawyer and a credit to the profession.

Heustis v. Heustis, Ky., 346 S.W.2d 778 (1960), a divorce case in which it was held that a wife who has not directly contributed to the money or property accumulated during the marriage should nevertheless be awarded a share of it in the form of alimony, and that if she has not brought on the divorce by moral delinquency, she should be awarded alimony in an amount equal to at least one third of the estate accumulated from the income of the husband during the marriage. This opinion reflects the growing attitude of the court that except in flagrant instances fault is not a sound basis for determining alimony. It foreshadowed the eventual enactment of a no-fault divorce statute (introduced by Senator Bill Sullivan).

Butler v. United Cerebral Palsy of Northern Kentucky, Inc., Ky., 352 S.W.2d 203 (1960), holding that the education of children for whose education the common schools are not adequate is a proper public purpose which can be carried out through the appropriation of public funds to private institutions. The most difficult legal question in this case was whether in delegating authority to the state school board the legislation had provided sufficient standards or safeguards, so we had to come to grips with the old bugaboo of "standards." We ended up by adopting the approach suggested by Kenneth Culp Davis in his treatise on administrative law, that if it meets "the practical needs of effective government," questions of basic policy may in some cases be better left to the administrative agency itself, and in this instance we concluded that the state board of education was better qualified than the legislature "to establish and carry out whatever further policies and procedures may be necessary or desirable." This was a substantial step forward in the field of administrative law. (As of this hour, however, in September of 2001, there is considerable complaint by members of the legislature that the administrative agencies of the executive branch are taking far too much leeway in adopting regulations. It may very well result in legislation designed to curtail that tendency. If I had it to do all over again today, I think I might find a way to reach the same result without saying that an administrative agency can make policy. That, I think, is better left exclusively in the hands of representatives elected by and directly answerable to the voting public.)

Lee v. Tucker, Ky., 365 S.W.2d 849 (1963), was a wrongful death suit arising out of an automobile accident in which both the driver and passenger in one of the vehicles were killed and there was no direct evidence to show which one of them was the driver. The plaintiff had the burden of proving that the defendant's decedent, who was the owner of the car, was the driver. One or more witnesses testified that shortly after the car left the town of Barlow on the way toward Paducah the owner was driving and the plaintiff's decedent (his daughter) was riding in the right-hand or passenger side of the front seat. A short time earlier, however, while the car was parked in Barlow, the daughter had been seen in the driver's seat. It was shown also that her father had a heart condition and she often did the driving when they were together. The accident took place some twenty miles up the highway toward Paducah. The case offered a propitious opportunity to delineate between presumptions and permissible inferences and to make a clear statement that burden of proof is established by the pleadings, and is not shifted by the evidence. Thus: The father's ownership of the car, and his having been seen driving it a short time before the accident, was sufficient to entitle the daughter's administrator to a directed verdict in the absence of at least some degree of credible evidence to the contrary. This is what we chose to characterize as a *rebuttable presumption,* which does not cast upon the defendant the burden of proof, but to avoid a directed verdict he must produce countervailing evidence that injects enough doubt that the jurors may reasonably conclude that the plaintiff has not proved his case to their satisfaction. If he does that, the rebuttable presumption theretofore enjoyed by the plaintiff has been reduced to a *permissible inference,* meaning that the jury *may* find that the father was the driver but is not *compelled* to do so. In this case, *Lee v. Tucker*, the jury found for the defendant (the father's administrator).

This use of the word *presumption* may not be in keeping with traditional definitions. However, when a party with the burden of proof produces a quantum of evidence that would entitle him to a directed verdict if it goes uncontradicted, under any other name it has he same effect, and the word *presumption* serves as a convenient definition. Frankly, over the years I have felt that this was one of the most useful opinions I have written.

Later on, in 1966, I had occasion to write an opinion in *Scott v. Patterson,* Ky., 400 S.W.2d 526, restating the principle discussed above as follows: "A party not having the burden of proof is not required to adduce 'substantial evidence' in support of his defense in order to avoid a directed verdict. It is only necessary that he muddy the water enough that it cannot be justly held that there is but one conclusion reasonable men could reach." *Id.,* at 531.

Sometimes when a judge employs the vernacular in an opinion it does not amuse the losing lawyer, and in this instance Pat Rankin, a fine lawyer in Lincoln County who had tried the case for the plaintiff and lost it, apparently did not much care for the foregoing figure of speech, a fact that I learned in this unusual manner: At a state bar meeting held at the Executive Inn in Louisville some time later – perhaps two or three years – my son, who had recently become a lawyer, laughingly told me that for the first time in his life he had heard me referred to as a son-of-a-bitch. In those days there were always a couple of hospitality rooms in which the lawyers gathered for drinks and camaraderie, and it was at one of these that he had heard Pat cussing me out for my opinion and choice of words in his case. I did not take offense at this – most any lawyer, and a judge in particular, is going to be called a son-of-a-bitch at one time and another, and he learns to take it in stride. The late, great Justice Robert Jackson, in his wonderful little essay in the *American Bar Journal*, "The County Seat Lawyer," suggested that after losing a case a lawyer has every right to go down to the saloon and broadcast his contempt for the judge. Cf. 36 A.B.A.J. 497 (1950). Anyway, as the years passed by I got to know and respect Pat Rankin, and we had an amiable relationship.

In *Pritchett v. Marshall*, Ky., 375 S.W.2d 253 (1963), involving the Department of Fish and Wildlife Resources Commission and the state Personnel Board, we had occasion to state two propositions which theretofore may not have been entirely clear. One is that Article 2 of the Kentucky Constitution, which forbids arbitrary power, is "broad enough to embrace both due process and equal protection of the laws, both fundamental fairness and impartiality." 375 S.W.2d at 258. (Incidentally, there is no comparable provision in the federal constitution, and I have always thought it has been greatly neglected by the lawyers of Kentucky. It is a beautiful concept.) The other is that even if a statute creating an administrative agency declares that there shall be no appeal from its actions, recourse to the courts is always allowable if there is a constitutional issue.

In *Corken v. Corken Steel Products, Inc.*, Ky., 385 S.W.2d 949 (1964), overruling previous authority to the contrary, we adopted the "positional risk" doctrine for workers' compensation cases. That is to say, if the injury or death would not have occurred except for the employee's presence at a place to which he had come by reason of his employment, it is compensable. In this instance the employee had stopped for lunch, and as he re-entered his automobile was shot and killed by a stranger acting without provocation or discernible reason of any kind. An earlier decision had held that under similar circumstances an employee's death did not arise out of his employment.

One of the most vexing rules of substantive law that seems to be cast up by the sea with changes in the tide is the doctrine of sovereign immunity. Aside from its origin and existence under the common law, Section 231 of the Kentucky Constitution provides that the legislature may say how and in what courts suits may be brought against the Commonwealth, and that provision has been construed as prohibiting any suit against the state or any of its agencies or subdivisions unless permitted by legislative action. Until 1963, however, suits against the state (the Department of Highways in particular) for breach of contractual obligations were considered to be permissible. Then came an abrupt change in the road. In *Foley Construction Company v. Ward*, Ky., 375 S.W.2d 392 (1963), with an opinion written by Judge Montgomery, the court overruled the previous cases so holding, and held (correctly, as I see it) that this defense applied in contract cases as well. This was an important case because, as a result, in 1966 the legislature enacted legislation authorizing claims against the state for breach of contract.

Watkins v. Fugazzi, Ky., 394 S.W.2d 594 (1965), was a case of considerable importance to the City of Lexington. The issue was whether the proposed method of financing its downtown urban renewal project was valid. At first our court declared it invalid, but on rehearing we held otherwise on a 5 to 2 vote. I wrote the prevailing opinion, having changed my own mind.

After the first opinion had been issued the movers and shakers of Lexington were able to get a substantial number of the most prestigious lawyers in town, featuring Bert Combs, to present an *amicus curiae* brief in support of its petition for rehearing and, as might be expected, an oral argument was allowed. It was held in our conference room, and I well remember it. I thought that the best argument, from the standpoint of logic and reason, was made by Earl Wilson. In any event, his was the argument that changed my mind, and it was largely around that argument that I wrote the opinion. I say this because later on, at a banquet honoring Combs, Mayor Fugazzi attributed this turnabout to their having brought him into the case. With all respect to Bert Combs, with whom I had a warm friendship for many years and until his death, his presence in the case was not the magic that induced the change, on my part at least. It was the simple, clear, explanatory argument made by Earl Wilson.

Of all the 900 to 1,000 cases in which I had the privilege of writing opinions, I liked the tort cases best. *Mackey v. Spradlin,* Ky., 397 S.W.2d 33 (1965), was one of them. In a 4 to 3 decision we held the operators of an ice cream truck liable as a matter of law for the death of a small boy who ran into the side of a passing dump truck as he tried to run across the street after having obtained an ice cream cone at the ice cream wagon. It was our opinion that the act of enticing a group of children to their wagon for the purpose of selling ice cream to them created a duty on the part of the operators to keep a lookout for approaching traffic and exercise reasonable care to prevent their being injured by approaching traffic. My old and good friend Joe Stopher tried this case for the ice cream vending company, and I know he strongly disagreed with our ruling, but I am still confident that we "got it right" as my revered colleague Brady Stewart (one of the dissenters in this case) used to say.

City of Ashland v. Heck's, Inc., Ky., 407 S.W.2d 421 (1966), was another one of those cases that raised a lot of brimstone and fire around the conference table. Some years earlier, in *Arlan's Dept. Store of Louisville v. Commonwealth,* Ky., 369 S.W.2d 9 (1963), we had upheld the validity of a municipal Sunday closing law and declared that a retail department store could not do business on Sunday as a "work of necessity." In the *Ashland* case we held, on the constitutional ground of equal protection (cf. *Yick Wo),* that the city could not enforce its Sunday closing ordinance against a department store without also enforcing it against other businesses.

Cullinan v. Jefferson County, Ky., 418 S.W.2d 407 (1967), written by Judge Montgomery, held that counties and county boards of education come within the constitutional protection of sovereign immunity. It continues to be a leading case today. I mention it here because of my dissenting opinion in it. Over the many years that have passed since *Cullinan* was handed down there have been numerous attacks on the doctrine of sovereign immunity, and the lawyers rarely fail to cite or quote from that dissenting opinion. The irony of it is that I changed my mind about it long ago. The reason I feel differently about it now is that after a great deal of reflection I have come to the conclusion that the root of the trouble is in the doctrine of *respondeat superior.* Although it may seem unjust that a person run down by a reckless driver cannot recover from the driver's employer if the employer is the government rather than a nongovernmental entity, where is the justice in holding the master liable for his servant's negligence in *any* case, assuming that the master had no reason to anticipate it? Why should an innocent employer be held liable solely because the accident happened in the course of the work he has assigned the employee to do? In the case of a governmental agency, why should the taxpayers be responsible? In the instance, for example, of an elected official, there will be taxpayers who did not vote for him and some who were not even citizens of his bailiwick when he was elected. That they will have to contribute to the satisfaction of his liability is simply preposterous. We have that very situation in Franklin County today. Although the doctrine of *respondeat superior* may sell a lot of insurance, I think the legal profession ought to reconsider it solely in terms of logic and justice.

In 1968 the court issued an opinion of great importance in the law of worker's compensation, holding that an injured worker's disability should be determined on the basis of the extent to which his over-all earning power has been impaired, regardless of his usual occupation or the degree of his *functional* impairment. Before that time the worker's disability was determined on the basis of his usual occupation. For example, it had been held in *Leep v. Kentucky State Police,* Ky., 366 S.W.2d 729 (1963), that a police officer was totally disabled if he could no longer do police work, even though he may have been able to find employment in a less strenuous occupation. The line of cases represented by *Leep* (which I had written) was overruled by *Osborne v Johnson,* Ky., 432 S.W.2d 800 (1968). The *Osborne* opinion was one of the best that I remember and was written by one of the ablest members of our court, Commissioner Robert K. Cullen.

Robert Cullen
Ca. 1970
Courtesy of Sally Cullen Bryan

In *Jett v. Commonwealth,* Ky., 436 S.W.2d 788 (1969), a criminal case, we held that an out-of-court statement made by any person who appears in the trial as a witness, which statement is material and relevant to the issues in the case, may be received as substantive evidence through the testimony of another witness, and need not be limited to impeachment purposes. This was a new rule in Kentucky and has been of much assistance to prosecutors. The essential facts of the case were that the defendant's wife had called the sheriff and told him that her husband was "fooling around with or taking advantage of" her little sister on the bed. The husband was indicted for detaining the sister against her will. At his trial the wife denied having made this statement (as so often happens in similar cases). The *Jett* case held that it was proper to allow the sheriff to say what the wife had told him on the telephone, the hearsay rule notwithstanding.

G. And in the '70's and '80's

Probably the most significant opinion I had the occasion to write in the field of tort law was *Orr v. Coleman,* Ky., 455 S.W.2d 59 (1970). The gist of it is that as between or among joint tortfeasors the burden of liability should be apportioned according to their comparative culpability. Previously, for example, the injured party could recover 100 percent of his damages from any one of two or more joint tortfeasors, whereas now the liability of the one sued is limited to his percentage of the causative fault, as determined by the jury. Hence a joint tortfeasor may settle with the claimant without fear of a suit for contribution by the other tortfeasor or tortfeasors, and a tortfeasor with 1 percent of the fault can no longer be forced to pay 100 percent of the damages. My respected friend the late Charlie Leibson, who came onto the court as I was leaving, never did like this result, but it has stood the test of time.

Kentucky Bar Association v. Tussey, Ky., 476 S.W.2d 177 (1972), was a *per curiam* opinion of which I was the author. Although the case was not one in which there would have been a great deal of public interest, it was of considerable significance to the legal profession. The issue was whether the preparation of real estate mortgages for a bank by one of its lay officers constituted the practice of law. We held that it did, and, therefore, that such a practice is impermissible. The defendant in the case, however, was not the bank, but one of its officers, and in view of the previous uncertainty of the law in this regard we declined to hold him in contempt of court. Ironically, though it had been argued that by sitting in judgment of a dispute involving its own creature, the bar association, the court was violating fundamental rights protected by the federal constitution, the fact that we did not visit any punishment on the defendant in the case had the effect of preventing an appeal to the federal courts.

As I recall, the oral argument for the bar association was made by Frank Logan, of Louisville, which provides an appropriate occasion for me to say that I think he was the most forceful and persuasive advocate I have ever heard. Some of the greatest lawyers in the state joined in presenting the defendant's brief, and I am confident that one of them did a fine job in the oral argument, but, sad to say, I just cannot remember who it was. One thing I do remember is that Bert Combs and the Wyatt-Tarrant firm were among the counsel, and in later years Bert twitted me now and then for having euchred them out of an appeal to the feds.

One other thing about that case ought to be mentioned. It gave us an opportunity to discuss the propriety of our sitting in judgment of a case involving the bar association, which was our own agency. It is an interesting question, the answer to which is, "Who else?" The same subject is pursued at greater length in the later case of *Ex parte Farley,* Ky., 570 S.W.2d 617 (1978).

In *Commonwealth Life Insurance Company v. Hall,* Ky., 517 S.W.2d 488 (1974), I again had the occasion to delve into the subject of presumptions and burden of proof (see previous discussion of *Lee v. Tucker,* at page 30). If you read the opinion, don't do it after two or three drinks, because it is pretty gummy and requires a clear head. After all these years of rusting I have a hard time staying with it myself. Anyway, it was one of these "accident or suicide?" cases in which the plaintiff had the burden of proving that her husband's death by a shotgun was an accident in order for her to collect under the double indemnity clause of his life insurance policy and the insurance company had the burden of proving suicide in order to defeat the claim entirely. There is a rebuttable presumption, for example, all other things being equal, that the deceased person did not commit suicide, so the party (in this case the insurance company) claiming that he did must prove it to the satisfaction of the jury. With respect to whether the death resulted from an accident, entitling the beneficiary to double indemnity, there is no "presumption" one way or the other, but the claimant has the burden of proving to the satisfaction of the jury that it did. (From a practical standpoint this is the equivalent of a rebuttable presumption *against* accident as the cause of death.) If the jury could not be convinced either way, the widow was entitled to recover the face amount of the policy but not the double indemnity. The instructions actually given failed to present that option, so that the jury was limited to an "all or nothing" choice between accident and suicide, which we found to be erroneous. The jury having awarded double indemnity, we reversed the judgment and directed a new trial. Even though I wrote the opinion, I think it has instructive value.

Discussion of the rubber dollar case, heretofore mentioned, would not be complete without including *Sarakatsannis v. Baker,* Ky., 488 S.W.2d 683 (1972) and *Commonwealth v. Hesch*, Ky., 395 S.W.2d 362 (1965). In *Sarakatsannis* (which was assigned to me) the legislative body of the City of Newport in 1970 raised the salary of its police judge, which had been $720 per annum at the time he took office, to $12,600 per annum. A dissenting member brought a suit contending that the ordinance was invalid. It was my opinion at first that the compensation of a public officer could not be increased during his incumbency to more than the current value of his salary at the time he took office. I still believe that should be the correct answer, but on a petition for rehearing I was tripped up by an earlier opinion written by Judge Milliken in the *Hesch* case, which had upheld a 1964 statute increasing the compensation of officers *then incumbent* to reflect the purchasing power of the 1949 dollar, rather than the purchasing power of the dollar as of the later dates on which those officers had assumed their current terms of office. If that case was cited in the original brief I must somehow have overlooked it, and certainly I should have remembered it anyway, but unfortunately I didn't, so I had to eat my words and write a new opinion. As it is, it seems that each time the rubber dollar question came up and Milliken had the case I don't remember the conference discussion. Having so often thought that Milliken lived somewhere in the clouds, I'll have to confess that in these instances I am the one who must have been there (or asleep). If it be said that *Matthews v. Allen,* the original rubber dollar decision, left salary limits in shreds, *Hesch* and *Sarakatsannis* swept the shreds away.

One of the newer theories of tort liability that loomed into prominence during my time on the court is products liability. We now have a products liability statute, KRS 411.300 *et seq.* Much has been written on the subject, and there has been a superabundant use of expert witnesses. Yet it is, I think, a rather simple concept that really ought to be understood better than it often seems to have been. Basically, strict liability means that if a product that proves to be unreasonably dangerous is put on the market and causes injury to its intended or expected user, the manufacturer or seller (subject to various exceptions) is liable. Liability does not depend on fault. It is just one of the costs of doing business, and harks back to the ancient rule that as between two innocent parties the one who created the occasion for an injury should be responsible for the consequences. In one of our first few of these cases, *Ulrich v. Kasko Abrasives Co.,* Ky., 532 S.W.2d 197 (1976), I undertook to simplify the theory of liability, so as to obviate some of the evidentiary complications. (Some, however, have been restored by the statute.) The point I sought to get across was that since liability depends solely on whether the product was or was not unreasonably dangerous, it should not make any difference whether it was properly designed or manufactured, or conformed to the state of the art existing at the time of its manufacture, or was made of defective materials, etc. As said in the opinion, "The product is or is not unreasonably dangerous to a person who should be expected to use or be exposed to it. If it is, it can make no difference whether it is dangerous by design or by accident." As in the instance of the onerous principle of *respondeat superior*, the law of products liability holds the manufacturer responsible regardless of his actual innocence.

Our present statute provides that a manufacturer may avoid liability if it can be shown that the product was manufactured in conformity with the state of the art existing at the time. KRS 411.310(2). It seems to me that this represents an effort to introduce negligence as a criterion of liability and is not consistent with the fundamental purpose of strict liability, which is to hold the manufacturer responsible for what he sells.

The *Ulrich* case brings to mind a fond memory of my colleague Scott Reed, the first Chief Justice of the Supreme Court (and my predecessor in that capacity) as so named by the 1975 Judicial Amendment. At the time I was working on this case an article came out in the *Kentucky Law Journal* in which Scott felt that his opinion in the earlier strict-liability case of *Jones v. Hutchinson Manufacturing, Inc.*, Ky., 502 S.W.2d 66 (1973), had been either misquoted or misconstrued, or both. He was mad as a hornet, and was threatening to write a letter, or perhaps a concurring opinion in *Ulrich*, chewing out the young student who had written the article. He was hot as a firecracker, but I finally managed to talk him out of it by assuring him that I would smooth it over in the opinion I was about to write – which I did. And when it was finished his feathers had settled down, and he was satisfied with it.

Scott Reed
Ca. 1978
State Photo

One of the most controversial cases, among the members of the court, that came to us during my tenure was *Fann v. McGuffey,* Ky., 534 S.W.2d 770 (1975), which involved the validity of the 1974 no-fault automobile insurance law, KRS 304.39-010 *et seq.,* and was decided on a 4 to 3 vote. I wrote the majority opinion, Scott Reed wrote a concurring opinion, and Bob Lukowsky added a dissenting opinion in which Pleas Jones and Marvin Sternberg concurred. It was a difficult, complicated case – too much so for me to undertake a summary here – but it had one comical aspect that is worth telling for the purpose of illustrating what goes on within the sacred precincts of an appellate court. The decision was handed down just before the court's summer recess. One of our most recently elected judges, Boyce Clayton, who had concurred in the majority opinion, heard so much grousing from the lawyers back home in western Kentucky that when we came back for the fall session in September and had received a petition for rehearing, he wanted to change his vote, which, of course, would have resulted in the law's being struck down. I don't know today how we got him to hold still and stay with the opinion, but I do remember that it wasn't easy.

The sovereign immunity doctrine arose again in *George M. Eady Company v. Jefferson County,* Ky., 551 S.W.2d 571 (1977), and again, as had been done in the 1967 *Cullinan* opinion, we pointed out that although the legislature had enacted a statute allowing suits against the Commonwealth, it had not seen fit to disturb the immunity of counties. As of this writing that condition still prevails, thanks to the reluctance of legislators to offend their fiscal courts.

Shortly after I had become Chief Justice in September of 1977 the state Public Advocate, two of his assistant counsel, and two likely candidates for death sentences filed suit in the Franklin Circuit Court against the Supreme Court and all of its members, including the Chief Justice, AOC and the Administrative Director of the Courts, and the executive assistant of the Chief Justice, individually and collectively, demanding that the plaintiffs be allowed to inspect and copy whatever records were being compiled pursuant to KRS 532.075(6), a subsection of the recently-enacted statutes relating to the death penalty. This, to say the least, was a most unusual proceeding, challenging the authority of the Supreme Court and its control over its own records. Rather than go through any *fol de rol* in the circuit court we simply entered an order removing the proceeding to our court and dealing with it in the form of an official opinion, *Ex parte Farley,* Ky., 570 S.W.2d 617 (1978), denying the relief. This opinion discusses a number of fundamental principles and, I believe, is one of the most important that I had the privilege of writing during my time on the court.

Grogan v. Commonwealth, Ky., 577 S.W.2d 4 (1979), arose out of the tragic Beverly Hills Supper Club fire in northern Kentucky. The action was brought by several injured parties and personal representatives of victims who had lost their lives in the fire, against the City of Southgate and the Commonwealth of Kentucky. The basic holding was that the failure of a governmental entity to enforce its safety regulations does not constitute a tort against individuals who are injured as a result of that failure.

Ex parte Auditor of Public Accounts, Ky., 609 S.W.2d 682 (1980), provided the occasion for the court to issue a judicial "bill of rights," and in which I assumed the prerogative of writing the opinion myself. For some time the Auditor of Public Accounts had wanted to audit the books of the state bar association, which customarily had employed a certified public accountant for that purpose and did not welcome an intrusion by the state auditor. In this instance the state auditor addressed a letter to the Chief Justice requesting that the question of his authority in this regard be resolved by the Supreme Court. We responded with a formal opinion holding that under the 1975 Judicial Amendment the judicial branch of the state government has exclusive authority to manage its own affairs, that the bar association is a part of the judicial branch, and that the auditor does not have and could not be given any legal authority with respect to the bar association. It was my friend and successor the illustrious Bob Stephens who dubbed this opinion as the "judicial bill of rights."

The last opinion of political interest that I wrote before the end of my final term on the court was *Brown v. Barkley,* Ky., 628 S.W.2d 616 (1982), in which the Commissioner of Agriculture challenged the validity of an executive order of the governor transferring various funds, functions and personnel of the state Department of Agriculture to another executive agency. The trial court held that the order was not authorized by the enabling statute pursuant to which it had been issued. Our court agreed with that conclusion but felt it appropriate to consider the further question of whether the governor nevertheless has constitutional power to effect such a reorganization regardless of an enabling statute. This subject entailed a rather lengthy analysis of the distribution of powers effected by the Constitution Kentucky, and our unanimous conclusion was that "when the General Assembly has placed a function, power or duty in one place there is no authority in the governor to move it elsewhere unless the General Assembly gives him that authority."

In the course of reaching this conclusion I wrote the following comment: "It is axiomatic that under our Constitution the General Assembly has all powers not denied to it or vested elsewhere by the Constitution." I believe that proposition is fundamentally correct. Obviously it means, and was intended to mean, that unless there is something in the Constitution, express or implied, to prevent it, the legislature is free to enact any legislation it sees fit to enact. However, for some odd reason – perhaps from pique at having lost the case – one of the lawyers on the losing team co-authored an article in the *Kentucky Law Journal* two or three years later characterizing this opinion as having sown "the seeds of bad law. Fortunately, however, the bad law was never harvested because the Court overruled *Brown v. Barkley's* troublesome *dicta*, albeit *sub silentio,"* in *LRC v. Brown.* See "The Separation of Governmental Powers under the Constitution of Kentucky: A Legal and Historical Analysis of *L.R.C. v. Brown,"* by Sheryl Snyder and Dr. Robert Ireland, 73 Ky.L.J. 233 (1984-85).

The *LRC-Brown* case came up just before I left the court and was considered and decided some time later, after four newly-elected judges had taken office. It is reported in 664 S.W.2d 907 (1984). Whereas the ultimate focus of the *Barkley* case had been on the power of the executive, the LRC case concerned the power of the legislature, and in particular the extent of its power (if any) to delegate to its creature, the LRC, the authority to do things that it could not itself do except while in session. As pointed out in the opening paragraph of the

LRC opinion (written by Chief Justice Bob Stephens), this had been described as a power struggle between these two branches of our state government. Obviously there was some real anxiety on the part of the governor's people and his lawyers that the legislature was making a serious effort to enlarge its powers at the expense of his own, and without a doubt some young Turks in the legislature were so inclined. Anyway, the Louisville Wyatt-Tarrant-Combs law firm which had represented the governor and lost in the *Barkley* case was in this one as well. I do not know who actually argued the case – I had no interest in the matter and was not there. Presumably, however, the author of the law review article either wrote the brief or made the oral argument, or both.

At any rate, in trumpeting his or their victory in the subsequent *LRC* case (grandiosely dubbing it "Kentucky's *Marbury v. Madison*"), it evidently behooved the author of the cutting remarks in the law review piece to vilify *Barkley* (and me) by ascribing to it the very construction that their adversaries in the *LRC* case had tried unsuccessfully to sell to the court. A reading of the *LRC* opinion at 664 S.W.2d 913 will suffice to illustrate the point: "These words, plus the following, are seized upon by appellants in their argument as proof that somehow, this Court has sawed off one of the legs of the tripod, *viz.*, that of the executive . . . The inference appellants draw from this language is that the General Assembly possesses all power and authority to act which are not specifically denied it by the Constitution and has the power to act in exercising those powers. It is argued that *all powers*, residual in nature, belong to the legislative branch. We do not agree. . . . We would in effect be eliminating the separation of powers doctrine. . . . Nothing in *Barkley* can be construed to deny the existence of the doctrine of separation of powers and the equality of the three coparceners in government. . . . The power referred to in *Barkley* is *legislative power and legislative power only."* In short, nothing had been said in the *Barkley* opinion that could reasonably have been understood to suggest that the legislature had any power to do through LRC anything that it could not do itself while not in session. Stated more simply, by providing for regular and special sessions the Constitution by necessary implication limits the legislature's authority to what it enacts during those sessions. And regardless of what counsel on either side (including the perpetrator of the offensive law review article) thought, nothing in the *Barkley* opinion could reasonably be construed to mean that the court regarded the legislature as a Lord High Everything Else (cf. Gilbert & Sullivan's *The Mikado*).

That was the language in the LRC opinion that the law review article claims to have had the effect of overruling, *"sub silentio,"* the "troublesome dicta" contained in *Barkley*. But what the court actually "overruled," if anything, was counsel's (and LRC's) erroneous notion of what we said or had meant to say in *Barkley*. The court's opinion in the *LRC* case consisted very largely of rejecting, indeed fighting off, LRC's insistence that *Barkley* meant something that the court did not agree it meant. And in any event, had the court intended to overrule anything that had been said in *Barkley* it certainly had no need to do it "sub silentio." Apparently the authors (or author – Prof. Ireland told me that he did not write the portion of the article to which I am referring) of the law review article paid no heed to the fact that *Barkley* had been a unanimous opinion in which the writer of the great "landmark" LRC opinion, Chief Justice Stephens, had been himself one of the concurring judges. Surely he ought to have been given credit for having understood what we were saying, and meant to say, in that opinion. The only person "troubled" by the "troublesome *dicta*" of *Bartley* seems to have been the author of the law review diatribe.

One more word about these cases and I am done. In this same law review piece the following comment was made: "The historical footnote is that this request [by LRC, to permit early submission of the case to the Supreme Court] was seriously considered by some members of the 'old Court.' There was even discussion of the old Court and new Court sitting *en banc* at oral argument and all eleven justices [including the four new members who had been elected in 1982] joining in the decision, a stratagem that had no apparent purpose other than permitting Chief Justice Palmore to author the opinion of the Court after the expiration of his term." 73 Ky.L.J. at p. 199. [Query: how in the hell could that be done?] It will be noted that the article does not identify the parties to this so-called "discussion." If there was ever such a preposterous discussion, it must have been by somebody who was not a member of the court. Certainly it was never suggested in my presence. The first time I ever heard the canard was when I read the law review article. Bob Stephens told me he had never heard of such a thing. Then one day I happened to be at a dinner party with the lawyer who wrote it, and I asked him where he had got such an asinine story. His answer was, "From Combs." That may have been the truth, but I should think that Bert Combs was far too intelligent a man to say that kind of thing even if he had heard it from someone else – unless, of course, he intended some psychological effect on the mind of the listener (which it may very well have had. However ingenuous he may have appeared to be, Combs was not incapable of subtlety.) In any event, it was a hallucination on somebody's part, and a bit surprising that a former president of the state bar association not only would swallow it, but stoop to use it in such a mean-spirited way.

H. The 1975 Judicial Amendment

A constitutional amendment adopted at the November 1975 election made profound changes in the structure of the Kentucky courts. It abolished county and quarterly courts, magistrates' courts, and city police courts and vested their functions in a new District Court. It renamed the Court of Appeals as the Supreme Court and created a new Court of Appeals as an intermediate appellate court. Except for the change in its name the old Court of Appeals was left intact, as were the Circuit Courts. All judges in all courts were required to be lawyers, elected by the people on a nonpartisan basis. All in all, the amendment went a very long way toward eliminating politics from the system (although, of course, to borrow some prayer-book phraseology, wherever two or three are gathered together, there will be politics).

Of equal significance, the whole system, including the offices of circuit court clerks, was unified and integrated, with the Chief Justice as "the executive head of the Court of Justice." Whereas formerly the biennial budget of the judicial system had been merely a part of the budget that is statutorily required to be presented to the legislature by the governor, the constitutional amendment provided that the Chief Justice "shall submit the budget for the Court of Justice and perform all

The genesis of the 1975 Judicial Amendment. Judge Palmore is shown with Gov. Wendell Ford during the signing of the Invitation to Citizens Conference for Judicial Improvement.

October 29, 1973
State Photo

other necessary administrative functions relating to the court."

Another profound change brought about by the judicial amendment was the creation of an Administrative Office of the Courts, without which it would not have been possible for the Chief Justice to carry out his new administrative duties. The staffing and organization of this office in a brief period of time was an almost superhuman undertaking. Fortunately, our first Administrative Director, William E. (Bill) Davis, a brilliant and dedicated young lawyer, was equal to the task, and as I look back over the years I think that his was the greatest individual contribution to the success of the new judicial system. AOC continues today as an effective organization, and certainly it is indispensable to the judicial system.

A detailed enumeration of the problems the court had to face

The court's work could be quite voluminous, especially prior to the adoption of the 1975 Judicial Amendment.

Ca. 1974
State Photo

in order to bring things into conformity with the new system would not be within the purpose of this narrative. Some, however, should not escape notice, and one of these was the necessity of revamping the rules of practice. Anciently, the rules consisted of a code of practice for civil cases and a similar code for criminal cases. Both were statutory – that is, created by the legislature and within the power of that body to change as it saw fit. By the time, however, that the constitutional amendment came along the legislature had recognized that matters of practice within the courts really were judicial rather than legislative in nature, and the old codes had been superseded by rules prescribed by the Court of Appeals. When I came onto the court Watson Clay was and for many years had been *the* authority on the rules, and was the author of a textbook on the subject, but he retired in 1971, and as chance would have it I more or less "inherited" the job of looking after the rules, with the exception of those pertaining to the practice of law and professional conduct, which fell to Judge James Stephenson, of Pikeville, who had been elected to the court several years before, succeeding Judge Ed Hill of Prestonsburg. First we had a set of temporary or transitional rules and then a goodly number of amendments to the pre-existing rules, all of which I drafted and then submitted to the full court for approval. One thing in particular I recall is that we tried to simplify the appellate process by substituting a less formal presentation of arguments (reducing the requirements of a brief to something similar to the present-day "Statement of Points and Authorities" and cutting down the time limits), but we found that the lawyers wouldn't like it. They wanted to do it the old way and with plenty of time to prepare those god-awful "briefs." I made the mistake of calling this proposed statement of points and authorities a "brief" rather than simply a "memorandum," because it really was to be in lieu of a brief, and it went down like the *Titanic*.

Prior to the amendment we had very few oral arguments, for the simple reason that they are too time-consuming and the court was and for many years had been a year and a half or more behind in its work – that is, we had a backlog that would put any haystack to shame. Fortunately, we were able to reduce that backlog to reasonable proportions by assigning a substantial part of it to the new Court of Appeals (with its 14 judges). Since that time oral arguments in both of the appellate courts have been the rule rather than the exception.

That we were now going to enjoy the luxury of routinely having oral arguments was the circumstance that had moved me to envision a new procedure in which, rather than having the lawyers submit their arguments in the form of full-bodied briefs and then orally covering the same ground before the court, we would have both the lawyers and the judges sit around the table, with the original record of the case, and discuss the issues until the judges were satisfied that they had heard enough to enable them to decide the case.

I hope that some day the bench and bar will come to something like this in order to reduce the time and expense of appeals, but there is one other impediment that is likely to persist: if the lawyers are going to submit in advance of their oral argument no more than a short, simple statement of what they expect to say and a list of the authorities they wish the members of the court to read *prior to the argument,* then it will be imperative for the judges to do just that. As it is at this day and hour, and was when I was on the court, some judges – perhaps *most* judges – depend on their clerks or staff counsel to do much of their work. Some of my colleagues of yore used what I called "cheat sheets," summaries made up by their clerks for use by the judge during oral arguments. Such a summary, of course, makes it possible for a judge to act as though he has read the briefs even if he has not. On a court consisting of seven or more judges there will always be at least one of this species. I doubt, however, if it will ever be permissible (or should be) for law clerks to participate in the oral argument of a case.

The evolution of the 1975 judicial amendment also is a bit beyond the intended scope of this narrative, but again, there were some things about it that did not make enough noise to be chosen for the history books but, I think, really ought to be mentioned anyway for the edification of those who were not there to see it all at first hand. It was organized as a grass-roots effort involving people from various walks of life all over the state. I had very little to do with it except that I was one of a small committee that went over in the beginning to the office of the late, great Wilson Wyatt in Louisville and persuaded him to head it up. Incidentally, he was one of the truly splendid and gracious men I have ever known. Years later, after I had retired and my portrait was presented to the court, Wilson did me the honor of preparing and offering the customary resolution. (This calls for another comment: During my time on the court nobody's portrait was presented and hung up in the hall while he was still living, but some of our successors were anxious to see their pictures on the wall – just as they wanted to write opinions in cases arising from their own districts, which had been generally taboo theretofore – and after several years of resisting it I finally gave in to my old friend Bob Stephens, who wanted it done while he was still Chief Justice.)

Anyhow, to get on with the story, I think the late Glenn Denham, of Middlesboro, was president of the state bar association while the thing was going on, and I remember our having a session in the conference room with the bar representatives to discuss what we thought should be in the proposed constitutional amendment. I knew very well that the folks in the county courthouses would not take kindly to having their little courts replaced by a new district court, and I believed that would result in a defeat of the whole thing. (I scarcely dreamed that they would be caught asleep at the switch, as it turned out.) So I suggested leaving the lower courts out of it. In his own gentlemanly way, Glenn said that if we did that, there really was not much use in trying to do anything at all. How right he was! And how wrong *I* was. That was one of the few great moments I'll never forget.

Another unforgettable development in the effort to bring about a new judicial system was the help that was received from Justice Tom Clark, who had recently retired from the United States Supreme Court when his son, Ramsey, was appointed Attorney General of the United States. This friendly, courtly gentleman from Texas spent a good deal

Retired U.S. Supreme Court Justice Tom C. Clark and Judge Palmore.
1975
State Photo

of time here giving freely and generously of his time and counsel. I came to know him rather well, and I certainly liked and respected him.

Talbot "Sandy" D'Alembert, who at this writing (2003) is president of Florida State University, also came to Kentucky and gave us his expert advice, despite being on crutches as the result of a motorcycle accident.

Then there was the draftsmanship. Again, I had no part in it, but I know who did most of the work and oversaw the rest, and that was Morton Holbrook, of Owensboro, another longtime friend and an absolutely great lawyer. Lastly, to finish it off, the committee employed Jim Amato, a prominent lawyer and citizen of Lexington, to oversee the election effort, and the rest is history.

I. Life and Times as Chief Justice

On the first Monday in January, 1976, what theretofore had been the Court of Appeals became the Supreme Court of Kentucky, and its seven incumbent members were duly sworn in by Hon. Henry Meigs, one of the judges of the Franklin Circuit Court, as members of the new court. Scott Reed, of Lexington, who was then serving as Chief Justice of the old court, was elected by acclamation as the first Chief Justice of the Supreme Court, for a 4-year term. He served amicably and well, but administrative work just was not his cup of tea, and in September of the next year he resigned as Chief, remaining, however, as a member of the court. Some time later he was appointed to the federal bench and was succeeded by Robert F. Stephens, former Attorney General of Kentucky and, before that, County Judge of Fayette County. I was elected to succeed Judge Reed as Chief Justice.

The events leading up to my election to this office were nothing less than weird. At that time the court consisted of Boyce Clayton, from Benton, Marvin Sternberg, from Louisville, Pleas Jones, from Williamsburg, Robert Lukowsky, from Ft. Mitchell, Scott Reed, from Lexington, James B. Stephenson, from Pikeville, and myself. We all knew that Scott aspired to be a federal judge and might well be leaving our court at some time in the near future, so there had been some talk about who would succeed him as Chief. I remember talking to Scott and telling him that I did not covet the office but would be for Jim Stephenson if he wanted it. I told Jim the same thing, and he said that he would be willing to take the job on. Then one day at conference, in September of 1977, Scott announced that he was going to resign the Chief Justiceship. Whether he had confided his intention to do this to any of the other judges I do not know, but it came as a surprise to me. Anyway, he set a time two or three days later for the election of a new Chief Justice. Later on – during the same day I think – Pleas Jones and Bob Lukowsky came to my office and asked me if I would take the office. I told them I had assumed that Jim Stephenson would be elected. However, they were quite firm in their opposition to Jim, and I got the impression that if I would not run, one of them would. So we talked about it for a while and I finally agreed to run if they were sure there would be four votes for me. Counting myself, we knew we had three, but we didn't know about Clayton, so the three of us walked over to his office to find out how he felt about it.

It so happened that during one of our regular court conferences some time before this Stephenson had jumped on Clayton and criticized him for having his law clerk do his work and not doing enough himself. So when we broached Jim's name to him his response was heated and immediate, something like "Hell no, I'd never be for Stephenson!" In short, he agreed to support me, so we had the necessary four votes.

Having previously indicated to both Scott and Jim that I would be for Jim, I went to Scott's office and told him what had happened. Then I walked straight over to Jim's office and told him that I had changed my mind, because some of the other judges were not agreeable to his being Chief Justice. In a somewhat chilly way he expressed his surprise, and that was the end of the conversation.

The election was held, I think, on the next day, in the conference room, with no one present but the seven judges. The next surprise was that Scott announced that he was not going to cast a vote. Then Pleas or Bob Lukowsky – I don't recall which – nominated me. After a dead silence over the course of the next few moments Stephenson said something to the effect that, "Well, I'll just nominate myself." Somebody – it may have been Clayton, but I am not sure – suggested that we vote by secret ballot, so Scott tore six strips of paper out of a yellow legal pad and handed them out. When the votes were handed back to him, he picked them up one at a time and read out the names written on them. The result was three for Jim and three for me. What a shock! We had lost one of our four votes!

In view of the tie vote the meeting was adjourned until such later time as somebody could come up with enough votes to win. Within minutes after I got back to my office Pleas and Bob came in wondering what had happened. They both assured me that they had voted for me, so we all went down to Clayton's office to see what he had to say about it. He also insisted that he had voted for me, so the four of us went to Scott's office. I told Scott that these three men were telling me that they had voted for me, and I knew that I had voted for myself, so something had to be wrong somewhere. Well, Scott reached down into his coat pocket and pulled out the votes. One by one he read out the names appearing on the slips and laid them on his desk for us to see. Each of us except for Clayton identified his handwriting on one of the Palmore ballots. Then we examined the three Stephenson ballots. Clayton looked at one of them and exclaimed, "That's my handwriting, but I voted for you, Jack!"

With four of the judges professing to favor me standing there in his office, Scott called the others and we repaired to the conference room for another election. This time, however, there was no secret balloting, and the election went according to Hoyle.

It has been more than a quarter of a century since that day, and I have speculated lots of time about what really happened. I have some suspicions, but no proof. Perhaps Boyce Clayton could provide the answer.

The Judicial Article provides that the Chief Justice shall be elected for a term of four years. Scott Reed was of the opinion that when the office is vacated before the end of the four years for which the Chief Justice has been elected, his successor takes over only for the unexpired portion of that four years. In order to avoid any question on the matter, we had another election in 1980, four years after Scott's election, but for the future we entered an order construing the Constitution to mean that whenever a Chief Justice is elected, he is elected for four years. Consequently, although I had been re-elected in 1980, when I relinquished the office in September of 1982 the election of my successor, Bob Stephens, was for a term of four years.

At this time the Governor of Kentucky was Julian Carroll, a native of McCracken County, and former Lieutenant Governor as well as Speaker of the House of Representatives. His extensive background and governmental experience, to say nothing of his unusually high intelligence and ability, were indispensable to the enactment of the mass of legislation that was necessary to implement the new court system. When history is written it should not be overlooked that the success we recognize today would not have been possible without the interest, understanding and help of this bold and resourceful friend. Julian was the last Governor during my lifetime who had the political muscle and finesse to control the legislature. As an example, during the first session of his administration he put a bill through that body eliminating the nefarious institution of professional bail bondsmen in Kentucky. As of this hour I am not aware of any other state that has been able to do that, though some have tried. This enabled the new court administration to institute its highly successful (and honest) pre-trial release program. Julian Carroll was its father.

Another example of the Governor's fine Italian hand was in seeing to it that the District Court would not be activated until the beginning of 1978, but the new Court of Appeals would begin immediately. The result (as intended) was that there were 14 instant vacancies in the Court of Appeals, to be filled by gubernatorial appointment, whereas the first members of the District Court would be elected by the people in November of 1977. Thus the governor was able to make 14 new political appointments and at the same time insure that the new appellate court would begin its work with competent

Judge Palmore, Earl Powell, Addie Stokely, and Gov. Julian Carroll.
1975
State Photo

judges.

Quite naturally, I think, everything did not fall into place without some degree of friction. It was and still is my impression that some of the members of the new Court of Appeals envisioned a greater degree of independence (and prestige, no doubt) on the part of their court than those of us on the Supreme Court considered as being consistent with the unified system intended by the Judicial Amendment. For a time, for example, they had their own administrative director, and, as I recall, there may have been some difference of opinion as to whether all of their opinions should be published. On the whole, however, it all worked out rather well, and eventually we appointed the Clerk of the Supreme Court, John Scott, as Clerk of both courts, and placed the administrative authority for the entire system under AOC. After the first Chief Judge of the Court of Appeals succeeded in gaining an appointment to the federal bench we never had any problems whatever with that court. To this good day I am grateful to John Hayes, the second Chief Judge, for his friendship and cooperation during all of the time we worked together. I mention this in particular because when I first became acquainted with Judge Hayes he was a circuit judge in Louisville, and on more than one occasion we had to reverse him for being too rough on criminal defendants. He was an old FBI agent and a strict law-and-order man. He did not have a great sense of delicacy toward criminals, but of course we were living in the wake of the Earl Warren decisions and often had to enforce rights with which we may not have been sympathetic. Anyway, at first I viewed John's accession to the Court of Appeals with some degree of misgiving, but I was wrong – just as wrong as I had been that day out in the Pacific in 1945 when we got word that Harry Truman was now the President. From the first day on John Hayes was a first-class appellate judge and splendid Chief Judge of his court.

The great cloud hanging over us when I became Chief Justice was the imminent advent of the District Court. Though I do not know it as a fact, I have always suspected that one of the reasons – maybe the big reason – Scott Reed decided to resign as Chief Justice was that he just did not want to face this big mess that was coming up in January of 1978. He was a gentle man, not altogether comfortable in battle. The passage of the Judicial Amendment in 1975 had struck the county judges with much the same effect as Pearl Harbor had struck the United States Navy. It came as a complete surprise, and most of them did not like it at all. They felt that somehow they had been cheated – if somebody had just warned them they could and would have avoided it. They were not bothered by the upper courts, but they sure as heck were not going to put up with this usurping District Court if they could help it.

So, when I came onto the bridge they were already out to sink the ship. Bumper-stickers reading, "DUMP THE DISTRICT COURT" were all over the place. When the first of January rolled around many of the new District Judges were not allowed to use the courtrooms of the county court houses. A news photo in the Barbourville paper showed Judge Lewis Hopper holding court in a tent. Judge Benny Dickinson brought a state trooper along with him to see that he got into the courthouse at Edmonton. At Warsaw, the day after a padlock had been unsuccessful in preventing Judge Bob Greene's entrance, some local malefactor filled the lock with glue. But that didn't work either. By dint of the excellence of their performance the new judges soon gained such public acceptance and approval that the opposition gradually faded away.

By reason of its place in the history of the state, the first court having been held at Danville, I chose to conduct a ceremonial opening of the District Court there. Although this was intended as a symbolical opening of the court for the entire state, I believe Scott Reed held a similar a ceremony in Lexington.

It occurred to me that since they owned the various courthouses in the state, the counties should be entitled to fair compensation for their use by the state courts. Hence we drew up a bill to accomplish that purpose, and I felt that this should go a long way toward healing the wounds occasioned by the loss of revenues from the old local courts. Through AOC we were able to calculate a fair rental value for the space used by the courts in each county and to demonstrate that the rental payments would offset or compare favorably with the lost revenues. I think this system accomplished the desired result. (They took the money.) Unfortunately, it was not possible to do this for the cities that had lost their police courts, because for the most part the new system did not need to use their courtrooms.

In my capacity as Chief Justice I made three "State of the Judiciary" addresses to the General Assembly, in 1978, 1980, and 1982. The problems we faced and the progress we made are set forth in these documents, for which reason I do not feel a need to summarize them here. By this time, of course, I think it is generally accepted that our court system has been a decided success. I have already said that the existence and excellent performance of AOC has had a large part in that accomplishment, but I do not want to leave the subject without a heartfelt tribute to the splendid judges of the District Court. It really was their performance that brought the public approval without which the success and good repute of the system would not have been possible.

What I am saying about the District Court I have said on many prior occasions, including my speeches to the General Assembly. I am proud to say that I have been its chief cheerleader. It is our most important court, for the simple reason that more people come before it, more people see it and hear about it, and more people know what it is. From the very beginning I have believed that the performance of this court – these judges – would be the key to the public's judgment of the system as a whole. And, happily, I believe it has proved to be so.

Ironically, my vocal support of the District Court – especially in recognizing its preeminent importance in the system as a whole – aroused a good deal of animosity on the part of some of the circuit judges, who for some reason felt that they were being belittled. At one meeting of the circuit judges, for example, a hare-brained judge from Lexington read a written protest to that effect, which moved me to respond that I had never heard such a bunch of shit in my life. Nobody joined in the protest, and I know that a good many of the other judges enjoyed my response. Actually, I always had a good relationship with the circuit judges, and I never doubted that most of them were my friends.

With the members of the legislature there were ups and downs, though for the most part they were very cooperative and friendly. The gap between the salaries of the district judges and circuit judges was much greater than it was between the circuit and appellate judges, and it was more or less a constant effort on my part to remedy this inequity. This seemed to offend some of the circuit judges and some of the legislators. Once when I reminded the members of the legislature that the Constitution required "adequate compensation" for the members of the judiciary some of the more vacant-minded of that august assemblage took the position that I was threatening to carry out that provision by judicial edict.

The most serious encounter with the legislature, however, took place when an attempt was made (or at least threatened) to put the members of the legislature into the judicial retirement system. Our system (Milliken's baby) had long been the object of great jealousy by a number of the legislators, and they wanted to get in it or have one like it. However, there were two substantial obstacles. One was that there did not appear to be any handy way to fund it unless they raided our fund, and the other was that the time served by the legislators during their formal sessions simply would not add up to enough years of service to provide a very substantial retirement base. I think this contest came to a head during the regular session of 1980 (though it may have been 1982). We had a room adjacent to the Chief Justice's office that we called the "bunker" because it was there that visiting judges gathered to watch the legislative sessions on a closed-circuit television set. The late Henry Pennington, Judge of the Boyle Circuit Court, who as a young officer had served on General Patton's staff in Europe, brought in a copy of a photo showing the good General, surrounded by Hank and his other staff officers, urinating into the Rhine River, which inspired us to adopt the word POE – standing for "piss on 'em" – as our motto. It was sort of an exciting time there in the bunker, and at one point I was goaded into announcing that I would resign if the legislature actually went so far as to dilute our retirement fund by putting themselves into the system. In any event, the crisis passed and cooler heads prevailed. The legislature finally came up with a separate system of its own, calling it the "Judicial Form Retirement System." Why it was called a "judicial" form I do not know, unless the purpose was to clothe it with an aura of legitimacy that some may not have thought it possessed. Certainly it did not resemble our system, because, whereas judicial retirement benefits are based on years of actual service and compensation, legislative retirement benefits are beefed up by "presumptive" or fictitious service.

During my time as Chief Justice, in 1979, we lost the services of Bill Davis as our Administrative Director. He was a devout member of the Baha'i faith and left to fulfill a commitment to teach for a year in Haifa, Israel. He was replaced by an attractive young man from Alabama named "Bo" Cole, who was working in Atlanta for the National Center for State Courts. Bo stayed with us for about a year before leaving to teach school at Samford University in Birmingham. At this point Bill Davis came home from Israel, and I had just about succeeded in getting him to resume his old job with us when he was offered such a fine job in San Francisco that he could not turn it down. He has had great success since that time and is now going all over the world helping foreign countries set up new judicial systems. Fortunately, he suggested that I give Don Cetrulo, who had been his assistant at AOC, a chance at the job, and I took his advice. Don proved to be perfect for the job, and he was our Administrative Director for the rest of my time as Chief Justice and for several years under my successor, Bob Stephens.

Speaking of Bo Cole, he and his attractive wife Jane came to a parting of the ways about the time he left AOC. Jane was then going to law school at U.K., and she continued on to finish at the top of her class and was accepted into one of the leading law firms in New York City. In the course of her practice there she became acquainted with Jack Welch, the notable CEO of General Electric, and they married. Unfortunately, they too came to a parting of ways over his having an affair with another woman, which led to a highly publicized divorce

The Kentucky Supreme Court, as constituted at the end of Judge Palmore's time as Chief Justice. From the left are Boyce Clayton, Calvin Aker, Marvin Sternberg, Palmore, Robert Stephens, John J. O'Hara, James B. Stephenson.
1982
State Photo

case. As I pen these words on the 4th of July, 2003, I see from the morning paper that the case has finally been settled and that Jane will come out of it with at least $15 million. More power to her! She is a great girl, and I am sure she deserves every penny of it.

One last accomplishment during my tenure as Chief Justice in which I feel a good measure of satisfaction was the selection of my successor in that office. That choice, of course, was made by the members of the court, and not by me, but I did have a hand in it. As the end of my term drew near I felt that the transition should be made in time for me to coach the new man along and get him off to a good start. Bob Stephens had not been on the court for very long, and I did not think he would want the job quite yet, but one day he came into my office to discuss the matter and ask my advice. My immediate reaction was that if he could round up enough votes he should go for it, so that is what he did. Up until that time I had been in sort of a quandary as to who might be chosen by the other judges, and I had not made a choice in my own mind. However, despite the short time he had been on the court I knew that Bob was a skillful politician and would get along well with the legislature and the chief executive. This was of great importance because there was still much to be done for the new court system, and their cooperation was imperative. I did not think anyone else on the court was as capable as Bob in this regard, and as I write this, looking back on his 16 years in that office, I think he did the job remarkably well. It is very doubtful that anyone else ever will be elected to four terms as Chief Justice.

One of the developments during my tenure as Chief Justice was the admission of television into our courtrooms. I was always in favor of this, because I never could see a logical difference between taking photographs and drawing words and pictures on a piece of paper, but many of the judges were suspicious of the idea. We discussed the matter a good deal in our court conferences, and I can recall one public discussion in Lexington in which I espoused the affirmative of the issue and the chief judge of the Fayette Circuit Court expressed a different viewpoint. Anyway, from time to time Tom Hardin, who was in charge of the photography department of the Louisville *Courier-Journal*, would come over to Frankfort and prod me about when we were going to let cameras into the courtroom. Meanwhile, of course, the Florida Supreme Court had pioneered the effort and had done a superb job of polling the effects of the experiment, with favorable results. So in due course Tom's persistence bore fruit and we decided to unleash the tiger in Kentucky. However, we did not make it mandatory, but left it to the discretion of the individual judges and courts themselves. In retrospect, this proved to be a wise stratagem, because it avoided the resistance that would surely have been incited by an effort to force our choice down the throats of the other judges. At that time, as I remember, the Jefferson County judges were mostly in favor and the Fayette County judges against, but over the course of time since then it has become generally acceptable, to the everlasting credit of Tom Hardin and the Florida Supreme Court. Incidentally, although I do not know how it is now, during my years on the court Florida had an excellent Supreme

Court, and from time to time I found persuasive precedents in their opinions. I had an especially high respect for Arthur England, who as I recall was Chief Justice of that court when I held the same office on our court. At the time of my last contact with him several years ago he had left the court and was practicing law in Miami. A funny story I remember about him and another fine colleague of his on the Florida court named Alan Sundberg was that when they were both running for reelection Arthur had a problem getting it across to his constituents in South Florida that he was Jewish and Sundberg had a similar problem convincing the crackers in northern Florida that *he* was not.

Along with all the procedural rules changes brought on by the new system, we decided that there really was not much sense in continuing the practice of having legal papers and documents prepared on paper different in size from the letter-size stationery used in the rest of the commercial world, so we ordered the change for all documents filed in legal proceedings. As usual, of course, there was some amount of outcry from those who thought the sky was falling. I recall, for example, a complaint from one of the lawyers in Frankfort that he would have to get new filing cabinets. I assured him that if the smaller-size files wouldn't fit in his old cabinets we might help him buy some new ones. The federal courts, reluctant perhaps to follow the lead of their perceived inferiors, declined to follow suit until fairly recently.

I reached the age of 65 in August of 1982, and the term for which I had been last elected as a member of the court was to expire on the first Monday of January in 1983. I had come to the conclusion that after 23 years on the court it was time to leave. I like to think that the judges of this country are children of the common law system. Most of our great principles of law originated in the courts and thus were fashioned by judges. It was Henry II who admonished his judges to make the law suit the customs and attitudes of the people. In order to do that, it was necessary that the judges have a good understanding of the people. That holds true today. To the extent that the legislative bodies fail to do it (and of course most of the law is simply beyond their ken), our judges of last resort still have a duty to keep the law abreast of the attitudes and aspirations of the people for whom it exists. The point of all this is that during the era in which I served as a lawyer and

The retirement reception. From the left, Carol M. Palmore, Judge Palmore, and newly-elected Chief Justice Robert F. Stephens.

1982
State Photo

judge I may have had a fairly good understanding of the people in this state and country, but I did not think in 1982 that I could envision what the generation or generations of strangers who would be here tomorrow might like, want or need. It would be something akin to stocking a grocery store for a bunch of people living on the other side of the world. That is why I thought it was time to make room for another generation of judges. Even Jefferson made some wrong calls, and I certainly am no Jefferson.

J. Odds and Ends

Much of the work of the court, and of the Chief Justice, makes for dull reading. However, some of the many events and occurrences during my time as Chief Justice that will never make the history books may nonetheless be of passing interest (or amusement) to the kind reader of this work.

Early after the election of the first batch of District Judges in late 1977, for example, the new judges lost no time in forming an organization, and it became all too apparent that one of its main purposes was to lobby for its interests, as the Circuit Judges had done through the years. Foreseeing that this would in all probability create frictions within the system, with the approval of the other members of the court I issued an order prohibiting all members of the judiciary from engaging in any lobbying activities with the legislative or executive branches of the state government without express authorization from the Chief Justice. The purpose of this so-called "gag order" was to see that the judiciary would speak with one unified voice, and it had just that effect. Some of the District Judges did not like it, and at one of our educational sessions a young judge from Northern Kentucky suggested that the order was a violation of freedom of speech, and asked what would happen if he did it anyway. I gave him a two-word answer: "Try it." He did not try it. Nor did anyone else. It was and is a good rule.

Incidentally, throughout my tenure as Chief Justice I enjoyed a warm and cordial relationship with the District Judges, and their association has honored me more than once.

As I have mentioned, under the new court system all judges are required to be lawyers. Since there are not enough District Judges for each county to have one, District Judges are authorized to appoint trial commissioners for counties within their districts that do not have resident District Judges, but these trial officers also must be lawyers. One of my early problems arose out of the fact that in one of the districts the judge had appointed a former police judge who had helped him get elected. The trouble was, however, that the appointee was not a lawyer, and one of the lawyers in the district raised a complaint about it. I immediately called the District Judge, of course, and advised him that he would have to cancel the appointment and designate a new trial commissioner. The judge objected quite strenuously, because he had promised the job in return for the appointee's support in his election. Although I don't think we had any hard feelings over this, I finally had to remind him of the Retirement and Removal Commission (another innovation of the new judicial system) before he reluctantly agreed to rectify the situation.

A comical little tempest arose over the use of a toilet in one of the county courthouses. This facility was located adjacent to the office of the circuit judge, and either by custom or an understanding with the fiscal court – I don't know which – it had come to be his private precinct. Then the county officials wanted him to allow some other officials to use it during the infrequent meetings of their group in the courthouse. His honor took great umbrage at such an imposition, and flatly refused to suffer it. Somehow the impasse landed on my desk, and after hearing from both sides I decided that it would not do any irreparable harm for us to accommodate the owners of the courthouse. The judge being still unmoved, I just had to tell him that the matter had been decided, and that he had the choice of announcing it himself or having me announce it. That was the last that I heard of it.

Fortunately, as I have said, I always had a pretty cordial relationship with most of the circuit judges. They knew, I think, that I had great respect for them. So even when we had little differences they did not result in any overt hard feelings. One time there was a vacancy in the Warren Circuit Court and the late Tom Hines was appointed to fill it. Tom knew more about steamboats than he did about law, and he had a difficult time making the transition from bar to bench. He had a wrongful death case over at Hartford, in Ohio County, and was looking forward to collecting a good fee (those good cases do not come along very often for the average lawyer), but the case had yet to be tried, and he was anxious to try it. Somehow it never occurred to him that now he was a judge and couldn't try the case himself. Apparently somebody wised him up and told him that he would have to get another lawyer to handle the trial (and share the fee). I was Chief Justice at the time, so Tom called me and said it seemed to him that since he was practicing the case before he was appointed as a judge, surely it would not be improper for him to finish it. He took it hard.

Another instance occurred at Franklin, in Simpson County, following the appointment of Joe Clark as circuit judge. Fortunately, this one did not involve me – what I know about it is strictly hearsay, but I would not tell it if I did not believe it. Joe was one of the most unique and unforgettable men I have ever known. I met him when I was running for the court in 1959. He was the county attorney of Simpson County and had been a Chandler supporter in the 1955 gubernatorial race. Simpson County was Chandler territory, and I was a Clements man, but somehow Joe and I hit it off right from the moment we first met. (The same was true with respect to the county judge and his wife, the Chauvins, whose distinguished son, Stan, a lawyer in Louisville, later became president of the American Bar Association.) Anyway, when Joe ascended to the bench he kept his old law office across the street from the courthouse and continued to do tax returns for people, as before. Some of the lawyers in town did not feel that this was quite cricket, and one of them, Roy Steers, went to Joe's office and apparently remonstrated with him to the point that Joe whipped out his pocket knife and chased Roy around the office and out the door.

Both of these colorful men have been gone for lo these many years. Roy was a peppery fellow himself, but Joe was a real eccentric. During my election campaign he took me around to places in Franklin that I would bet no other candidate ever thought about. Joe owned a Rolls Royce automobile (naturally, the only one closer to town than Nashville), and when they had a sesquicentennial celebration in Franklin some years later I rode with Joe in the Rolls Royce in the parade.

I have fond memories of Franklin. The most beautiful courtroom was in Russellville, but Mrs. Chauvin saw to it that the courthouse yard in Franklin was surely the prettiest in all of Kentucky. And having mentioned Roy Steers, who also helped me in my campaign, I need to say a word or so about his lovely wife, Dorothy, who ran his office and knew more law than many a lawyer (perhaps including Roy). There was a time in my life that my wife did my secretarial work, and I realize what a treasure such an office companion is. I have much admiration for Dorothy, and share her pride in her son, Lee Steers, who was a little fellow back then but has since become a successful lawyer and Commonwealth's Attorney of his district.

One of the most constructive accomplishments that took place during the latter years of my time on the court and as Chief Justice was the building of the new Kentucky Bar Center in Frankfort. My particular connection with this had to do with the financing. Over the years, by statute, dues collected by the bar association from the lawyers were turned over to the State Treasurer, and were paid out by him (or her) as required by the bar association. At the time the bar association was considering the financing and construction of a headquarters building there was a large surplus of its funds in the coffers of the State Treasurer. It seemed to me that there was no legal or justifiable reason why these funds could not be used for this project. The Treasurer, however, was dubious as to his authority to let the bar association have the money, so I suggested that henceforth all dues collected by the bar association be deposited in its own bank account and that all of its expenses continue to be paid out of its funds in the hands of the Treasurer until those funds were exhausted. It was, and is, my opinion that under the new judicial article of the Constitution the bar association, as an arm of the court, is not required to bank its funds with the State Treasurer. In summary, the effect of this stratagem was to free up a substantial amount of money for the new building and make it easier for the bar association to arrange the necessary financing for the project. Happily, ground was broken for our magnificent bar center while I was still Chief Justice.

One of the funniest cases that was assigned to me while I was on the court involved the late Roscoe Tartar, who was then the judge of the Pulaski Circuit Court. It seems that during the winter, when it was cold outside, some of the "street people" of Somerset found it more comfortable to relieve themselves on the floor of the courthouse hallway, much to the annoyance of the fiscal court, which was in charge of the building. The fiscal court decided that the best way of dealing with the problem was to lock the courthouse doors every night. But whoa! Some of the folks did not like this ugly turn of events, and the dissenting members of the fiscal court appealed to the circuit court, contending that this violated the rights of the jailer, whose hostelry for the wayward was located on the second floor of the courthouse. His eminence the circuit judge most vigorously agreed, and supported his judgment with a philosophic opinion observing that when a person has to go, he or she just has to go, and is entitled to have a place to do it. For the interested, our opinion reversing this judgment is recorded in *Pulaski Fiscal Court v. Floyd,* Ky., 374 S.W.2d 683 (1964). Though not copied in our opinion, Judge Tartar's judgment is in the appellate record.

Judge Tartar, an uncle of the great John Sherman Cooper, was a colorful figure indeed. A story I heard about him was that one time he and a friend went up to Cincinnati – perhaps to see a baseball game – and as they were walking along the sidewalk of the street next to Fountain Square there were lots of other people coming and going, and Judge Tartar was tipping his big homburg hat and speaking to all of them – as he probably would have done in Somerset. When they reached the end of the block the good judge turned to his friend and said, "You know, we're getting a mighty good reception up here!"

I have some good memories of lawyers in Somerset, and there

have certainly been a lot of fine ones there. Swede Blackburn and his wife were delightful people. I think Swede was president of the state bar association when he suffered a fatal heart attack during the association's winter meeting in Costa Rica. The late Meriel Harris, one of the finest people I have had the privilege of knowing, had been my best friend back when he and I and Wendell Butler were in school at Western, traveling around the state with the glee club and that wonderful man the late Kelly Thompson, who at that stage of his career was the college publicity director. One time Meriel sang "The Road to Mandalay" in chapel and somehow got started off in a different key from the piano. I'll never forget it. It really was comical. I think at first he tried to fight it out by singing louder, hoping perhaps that the piano would eventually get in tune with him, but of course it was hopeless, and finally he just had to give up and start over, this time with the piano rather than against it. (I know this is not relevant to my career as a judge, but it is relevant to the memory of my old friend.)

In my early days on the court I came to know two memorable lawyers in Somerset who will be remembered, probably, for their bibulous camaraderie. One was Fritz Krueger and the other was Don Cooper, brother of John Sherman. Fritz was a big, hearty man with an infectious, bubbling personality. Don was a more intellectual type, a master of words. I had a great liking for both of them, and enjoyed their good company on several occasions, especially during bar meetings in Louisville. Don once paid me the high compliment of saying that he liked my opinions because I was "literate." I like that a little better than the choice of words my beloved old English teacher the late Frances Richards, once used when she said that as a student I had a "flair for words." Well – I reckon.

I guess that alcohol played its part in the demise of both Fritz and Don, but they were lovable guys while they were here, and I remember them fondly. I recall that once when I was in Washington at the National Airport waiting for a plane and talking with John Sherman Cooper, who was there for the same purpose, I asked him how Don was getting along, and his cryptic response was, "I guess Don's having a good time." God bless you, Don.

K. The 1963 Governor's Election

During the 1959 election primary, whenever Bert Combs came into the 16-county district in which I was running for the Court of Appeals I generally rode with him and we made what might be called joint appearances. Through the years thereafter, and until his untimely death, we were pretty good friends. One Sunday morning a year or two later, when he was Governor and I a member of the court, he called me at home on the telephone and asked me if I would like to ride up to Pikeville with him to attend a Bevins family reunion. Naturally, I was glad to go, though when I looked down from the state plane at that old Pikeville airport down in the valley I sort of wished that I hadn't. When we got back to Frankfort that afternoon he asked me to stay and have some snacks and a drink or two in the patio behind the mansion before I went home. Combs was a long thinker, and of course the discussion we had that afternoon was the reason he had asked me to go with him to Pikeville in the first place. (Among other things, he made me get up and say a few words at the reunion – interloper that I was – from which I now deduce, after all these years, that he wanted to see if I could speak to a strange crowd.)

The subject of the conversation was the next Governor's race. He was casting about for a candidate he could support, and suggested that I consider it. He mentioned several other possibilities and ticked off the pros and cons for each. I distinctly remember his saying that he believed John Watts wanted it, but he was not going to be for him. He did not say why. He said that Ned Breathitt would be a good candidate, but did not have an office he could use as a springboard. Henry Ward, of course, always had the itch to run, and, having been a newspaper man, stood to have the backing of the press, especially the *Courier-Journal*, but obviously Combs didn't think he could win. He thought the court was a good source for gubernatorial material and that I would be a good candidate, with the principal drawback being that it might be too soon for another member of the court, considering that he had come from the court himself.

Now let me make this perfectly clear – I was very happy as a member of the court, and I had no interest whatever in running for governor. Combs, however, had been both, and I remember his saying that being a judge was all right, but you could do so much more as governor. Anyway, I reluctantly agreed to let him have somebody arrange some public appearances for me, though of course I could not make any political speeches so long as I stayed on the court. In due course an attractive young man who worked for the state revenue department was given the job of scheduling appearances for me before various civic clubs around the state. His name was David Whites, and he had been the youngest county judge in the history of Lawrence County. Unfortunately, he was an inveterate alcoholic and carried a fifth of 100 proof Bourbon whiskey (Yellowstone) around in his brief case. This was his daily consumption – one fifth per day – but I must say that I never saw him when he showed any indication of being under the influence. We traveled on a state plane with a state pilot, and I spoke to a number of organizations from one end of the state to the other. As I could not talk about politics, I chose to speak on the historic role of courts in the development of the law. (Years later Combs told me that Mr. Robert Caldwell, an influential and very conservative Republican lawyer in Ashland, construed my remarks as meaning that I favored having the courts make the law – he did not seem to realize where the common law came from.)

Meanwhile, Ned Breathitt was actively and openly campaigning, and eventually Combs put him on the Public Service Commission. Some time in the middle of the winter of 1961-62 I spoke in Marshall County – I think it was at Calvert City – and Breathitt had spoken in the county the night before, probably at Benton. The county officials there (one was the brother of Shelby McCallum, later to become Speaker of the House during Breathitt's administration) were very much in Ned's camp, and were quick to tell me that right after his speech the previous evening he and Combs had talked on the telephone and Combs had virtually assured him that he was going to be the candidate. At the same time, I had been hearing that Ned's wife, Frances, was telling people that he was going to be endorsed by Combs. So, when I got back to Frankfort after that trip I went down to the governor's office and told Combs I didn't want to be a candidate anyway and would like to announce my withdrawal from further consideration. Among other things, I told him what I had been hearing in western Kentucky. He was very much opposed to my withdrawing, and disavowed having made any decision in Ned's favor. He assured me that what I had heard to the contrary was merely hopeful speculation, regardless of what people's wives might be saying. "Keep your powder dry" were his words to me. I agreed to keep my powder dry on one condition, which was that if and when he decided the other way he was to let me know first, so that I could take myself out and avoid the public posture of being passed over. We did not sign a contract, but I assumed that this was understood. Several months later I learned from the newspaper that Breathitt was to be the candidate.

Except for the fact that I had wished to take myself out of the race before another choice was announced, and was shocked that I was not given the opportunity to do so, I really was not disappointed. After all, I never wanted to be in it in the first place. I never, ever had any "fire in the belly" to run for governor. I liked being a judge. Even today I would rather be on the United States Supreme Court than to be President. Also, I had known Ned Breathitt and his law partners in Hopkinsville for a long time, and they were my friends. There has never been any envy or bitterness on my part toward Ned as a result of our temporary political rivalry prior to the 1963 election. Frankly, I was relieved and glad to be out of it. My only regret was for the loyal friends I had made and who were disappointed.

A funny thing happened during the time I was a "candidate" (or stalking-horse, as the case may be). One day while I was working in my office I had a telephone call from Earle Clements, who asked if I would be willing to talk to Mr. Bob Watts, the chairman or CEO of the Kentucky Utilities Company. (I assume that Mr. Watts, aware of my friendship with Senator Clements, had asked him to contact me.) Anyway, I said okay (what else?), and I went over to Lexington to see Mr. Watts, whom I had never met. I had no idea why he wanted to see me, and it turned out that he wanted to tell me the history of Fern Lake, a water impoundment in southeastern Kentucky that he had been instrumental in creating and was quite anxious to protect. As I discovered, it was involved in a lawsuit then pending in our court. Anyway, we had a long talk about other things, in the course of which he asked me who was behind my "candidacy" for governor. Actually I had no substantial backing, at least from a financial standpoint, and when I told him that my principal impetus was coming from Combs he gave me a piece of fatherly advice, something to this effect: "Judge, don't be fooled. They've already picked their candidate. When you get ready to run for governor, do it on your own. You'll be able to do that if you want to, but don't wait for somebody else to pick you and make you their candidate." In other words, be your own man. I shall never forget this good advice given to me by that wise and kind old gentleman. Incidentally, he only smiled when I asked him who "they" were and who was their candidate. But he knew.

Another incident that took place along about this time involved Clifford Smith, whom I have mentioned previously as a chief supporter of Happy Chandler. Evidently he was now ready to jump ship and enlist with Combs. So Combs came up to my office one day and asked me if I wouldn't talk to Mr. Smith and see if I could get his support. I told him, however, that I could not do this, because Mr. Smith frequently had cases in our court. In fact, KU was one of his clients, and may very well have had a case in the works at that time. So Bert asked me to see if Brady Stewart would do it, but Brady's reaction was the same as mine. He did not feel that it would be wise for him to do it. Thus in due course Mr. Smith gave his support to Ned.

One other thing I ought to mention before leaving this subject is that I did have some misgivings about what kind of a campaign I would conduct against Happy Chandler in the event I became the actual candidate of the Combs faction. Combs had a low opinion of Happy, and I figured that I would be expected to run him down pretty badly once we came to grips. Yet I really did not want to do this – and didn't intend to, either – because for one thing I regarded him as an elder statesman and entitled to a good deal of respect from a younger person like me. After all, he had been governor twice and was a great public figure in Kentucky regardless of political differences. It was my intention to focus mainly on the idea that he had had his hour (hours, I should say) on the stage and it was high time to make way for a younger generation. (Incidentally, in later years he and I became great friends, and he strongly urged me to get into the race when Combs and my old friend Wendell Ford were running against each other. That, however, for every reason I might dream up, was something I could not do.) It will be remembered, too, that in the 1963 contest Earle Clements, bitter at Combs for having fired him as Highway Commissioner following the notorious "truck deal," did the unthinkable by supporting Happy, much to the dismay of such old friends as Doc Beauchamp, Lawrence Wetherby, Clarence Maloney, Ed Pritchard and others. Earle had been my political benefactor and friend, and as I reflect on it today I think I simply should have firmly said no to Bert in the first place. I can't imagine what it would have been like to run for office with Earle on the other side.

L. A Word About Politics

At the time I ran for the Court of Appeals in 1959 my 16-county district extended in something like an hour-glass shape from several counties along the Ohio River to several along the Tennessee border. I had grown up in Bowling Green and had a good many friends and supports in Owensboro. These two cities being the most heavily populated in the district, they were vital to my political viability. Union County, adjoining my home county of Henderson, was the most westerly county in the district, and along about 1973 or 1974, when an eastward gravitation of population necessitated a legislative redrawing of the district boundary lines, it became distinctly possible that both Union and Henderson counties might be put in the First District, which extended westward to the Mississippi River and included such well-populated centers as Paducah, Hopkinsville, Madisonville and Mayfield, where I was not so well-known. So, in order to be sure of preserving my political base I moved my official residence from Henderson to my cousin Larry Depp's home in Owensboro. (I had long since sold my home in Henderson and was actually living in Frankfort. Commuting back and forth did not make for a satisfactory existence.) Meanwhile, I did sound out some of my lawyer friends in Madisonville to see whether they would support me if Henderson were put in their district, and I was gratified by their favorable reaction. As it turned out, in the eventual redistricting both

Union and Henderson were kept in the Second district, but anyway, my move to Owensboro may have tended to discourage any possibility of opposition from there in the next election, and it definitely avoided the prospect of running against my fellow judge Earl Osborne in the First District.

Political developments sometimes bring about gut-wrenching choices when two of your friends run against each other. This happened to me when Bert Combs and Wendell Ford ran for governor in 1971. Bert had been appointed to the highly prestigious federal Sixth Circuit Court of Appeals in Cincinnati and had served for some years on that bench, but for some reason or other had become tired of it and thought he might like to have another shot at being governor. (His fellow-judge John Peck once told me that it was a dull job and that he had far more enjoyed being a federal district judge in Cincinnati.) Wendell, on the other hand, had survived the Henry Ward-Louie Nunn debacle and as lieutenant governor was the highest-ranking Democratic state officeholder in Kentucky. He had not place to go but up, and it was the rightful turn to run for governor, which had always been his ambition. But there was his old compatriot Combs, up there in his plush seat as a federal judge, floating strong hints and rumors (but never saying for certain) that he, Combs, might run.

Bert Combs was noted for holding his cards close to the vest. This time it cost him the election. Ford did not want to run against Combs. Up to that point they had been political allies. Ford had served for a time in Combs' cabinet, until he went home to Owensboro to launch his own political career. It may be that Combs wanted to hold on to his federal job (and salary) as long as possible, because a public announcement that he was going to run for governor would have required him to resign.

Anyway, had he forthrightly communicated his intention (and in my opinion that intention was there all along) at a more timely stage of the game he probably could have had the nomination without opposition. This is not mere speculation. My source of information on that point was J. R. Miller himself, Wendell's closest adviser and political supporter. A short time before Wendell cut the Gordian knot and threw his hat in the ring J. R. told me that if Combs didn't come on out and declare himself Wendell was simply not going to wait any longer. So that is how it happened. I have never discussed this with Wendell, but I had seen something of this side of Bert back in 1961 and 1962. He was not free with his thoughts. It simply was not in his nature to reveal a decision until the last possible moment. This time it proved to be too late.

Combs and I had been warm friends since 1959, and I hated to see this race. Frankly I thought he would win (I did not foresee the adverse public reaction that would result from his giving up a lifetime office as a federal judge and wanting to be governor again), but in any event I could not turn my back on J. R. Miller and Wendell Ford. They had helped put me where I was, and they most certainly were my steadfast friends. So I quietly voted for Wendell Ford. My wife Eleanor, on the other hand, was for Combs — not that she had anything against Wendell, but we had been close to Bert and enjoyed his company on many occasions, both while he was governor and during his time in Cincinnati. It was almost as if he were a member of our court family. He never knew (nor did Eleanor) that I did not support him that last time he ran for office. Sometimes, being a judge is a blessing in that it provides a good excuse for keeping one's mouth shut.

I mentioned that Ford had once served in the Combs cabinet. There is reproduced on page 9 of this little narrative a photograph of Doc Beauchamp, Clay Wade Bailey and myself sitting together at a party given for Wendell on the eve of his departure for bigger and better things. Although I certainly was not one of his advisers or counsel, of course, I was among those of his friends who believed that if he was going to run for governor some day he needed first to win an election for some lesser office in order to demonstrate his electability. The state senator from Daviess County at that time was "Cap" Gardner, an insurance man in Owensboro, a person with a fine appearance and considerable personal charge, and he had ample political support. He was no easy pickings, but he was a Happy Chandler man, thus an enemy, and Wendell had the guts to take him on and beat him. You know the rest — lieutenant governor, governor, four times United States Senator. He did not come by those things the easy way.

The inauguration of Gov. Wendell H. Ford on the steps of the State Capitol. J. R. Miller (background wearing eyeglasses), from the left, Steve Ford, Gov. Ford, Jean Ford (behind governor's sleeve), retiring Gov. Louie B. Nunn, and Judge Palmore.

December 7, 1971

M. Instructions to Juries

When I came onto the court there was a three-volume work called *Stanley's Instructions to Juries* that was used by most of the lawyers and judges in Kentucky as a form book for jury instructions. The author was Osso Stanley, who was and for some long time had been one of the four commissioners of the court. Judge Stanley was a great reader and probably had a more thorough command of the English language and law in general than anyone else on the court. In addition, he was its most gifted writer. I suspect that more of his opinions were published in the *American Law Reports* (ALR) than have those of any other judge who has served on the Kentucky court. I really felt something like a novitiate coming to worship at his feet. He was a devoted Methodist and an equally faithful teetotaler. He did not smoke or drink. It was said around the court (perhaps jokingly) that when Stanley got a case in which one of the parties had been drinking you could bet on who was going to lose.

Judge Stanley had always wanted to be a regular judge on the court rather than a commissioner, but he was a staunch Republican, and his home district (he was a native of Bardstown) at that time was predominately Democratic. However, during the administration of Governor Simeon Willis, the last Republican to serve in that office until Louie Nunn was elected in 1967, Judge Will Fulton, of Bardstown, the Democratic judge then serving from that district, resigned his office, thus creating a vacancy to be filled by appointment. Judge Stanley hoped that Governor Willis would appoint him, but unfortunately for some reason Mrs. Willis, a very strong-willed woman, did not like him (or so I have been given to understand), and the governor appointed Clyde Latimer instead. The Stanleys were bitter, and I am sure that they never did forgive either of the Willises. All of which leads to the little story I am about to tell. One night Judge and Mrs. Stanley took me to dinner at the old Southern Hotel on Second Street in Frankfort, and while we were eating and talking ex-Governor and Mrs. Willis entered the dining room, whereupon Judge Stanley immediately said to Mrs. Stanley, "Here comes Sim Willis. Let's don't speak!" And they didn't.

The examples contained in *Stanley's Instructions* did not purport to be instruction forms prepared by Judge Stanley himself, but had been copied from instructions actually given by the trial courts in cases that had been brought before the court on appeal. In most of those cases, however, the court had not been called upon to consider the correctness of the instructions, and its decisions had been made on the basis of other issues. Hence in numerous instances they were not really authoritative, but were simply specimens of what had been given by the trial courts in various cases in which the record had been sent up to the court for its consideration on appeal. They were not examples of what Judge Stanley would himself have drawn. Some were good, some were bad, and most were indifferent. In Section 868, for instance, paragraph 1 of the instruction on murder requires the jury to believe beyond a reasonable doubt that the defendant "wilfully *and not in his necessary or apparently necessary self-defense"* (italics added) shot and killed the deceased party, thus placing the burden of negating self-defense on the prosecution, whereas paragraph 3 of the same instruction correctly places the burden of proving self-defense on the defendant.

Another important feature of *Stanley's Instructions* consisted of the footnotes appearing under each section. In fact, it would seem that keeping these footnotes up to date must have been the most onerous part of Judge Stanley's work on the book, because he footnoted everything relating to the subject-matter of the case rather than confining the footnotes to cases involving instructions. As a result, the work had assumed the proportions of a comprehensive text-book organized according to the list of instructions it covered.

Judge Stanley died in 1963, and not long afterward his publisher, The W. H. Anderson Company, of Cincinnati, asked me to take over the work of keeping *Stanley's Instructions* up to date and eventually revising it. Needless to say, I was greatly flattered to be chosen to succeed such an illustrious scholar and author, and of course I accepted the honor.

It was not difficult to prepare periodic supplementary publications in the form of new footnotes, but as I got into the matter of revising the work as a whole I finally came to the conclusion that the best thing to do was to throw the whole thing out and start from scratch. My objective was to present sample instructions in a clear and concise form for all types of cases that would ordinarily be expected to arise in the trial courts, and to present specimen instructions that I would consider to be correct. I also wrote up a new introductory text on the subject of instructions and continued with commentary and case notes following each example. It took several years to do this, and I started with instructions for civil cases. Meanwhile, however, the legislature authorized the drafting of a new codification of the criminal law, and I had the great pleasure of serving on the committee that met periodically with the drafters and passed on their work. When it was finished, the legislature, after making various changes, enacted it as the Kentucky Penal Code, effective January 1, 1975.

As this complete change in the criminal law loomed up over the

A meeting of the Penal Code Advisory Committee. From left, Judge Palmore (chairman); Sy Ramsey (A. P. Reporter); unidentified man standing; Frank Haddad, W. L. Matthews, and Pleas Jones.

December 4, 1969
State Photo

horizon it was imperative that we get up a new set of instructions for criminal cases, pronto. So I set aside my work on the revised civil instructions and got Bob Lawson to help me prepare a new volume on criminal instructions, which was published in October of 1974. Of course Bob needs no introduction here. A noted scholar, teacher, adviser and later dean of the University of Kentucky Law School, he had been a principal drafter of the new penal code and a member of our Interim Committee which reviewed the work as it progressed. Some years later I turned over the work on criminal instructions to Justice Bill Cooper, of Elizabethtown, my successor on the court.

The first volume of my revision of civil instructions, covering negligence only, was published in 1977, and a last volume, covering intentional torts and other civil wrongs, was published in 1989. In the preparation of this last volume I had the assistance of Professor Ronald

Eades, of the University of Louisville School of Law (now Brandeis School of Law). I kept up the supplements of this work until the year 2000, when I persuaded Don Cetrulo, former Administrative Director of the Courts, to take over.

The drafting of jury instructions is not a simple matter, even with the help of a form book. As people have different facial features, so do cases differ, one from the other. A proper drafting of instructions requires a careful analysis of the facts and the issues they present, and the burden of proof on each of those issues. A competent lawyer will do this well before he goes to trial. It is absolutely essential to an understanding of the case. You cannot just pick up a form book and put your finger on what you want. Yet some lawyers try to do that. More than once I have heard a lawyer say, after failing to shove a square peg into a round hole, "But that instruction came right out of your book!" Yes, but it didn't fit his case.

After I had become an octogenarian some time ago I decided it was about time for me to pass the instructions work over to younger hands. It was hard to do, because it had become a part of my life and, whether it was really so or just a figment of wishful thinking on my part, I always felt that I was doing something of help to the circuit judges, who try the major cases and have to give the instructions. The judges who try jury cases have a tough job. I don't believe most people realize how tough it is. I hope that I have been of some help to them.

CHAPTER 3
THE BROAD FORM DEED CASES

Because the ongoing controversy that culminated in the 1988 constitutional amendment reconstruing the "broad form deed" erupted on several occasions while I was a member of the court I have decided to say my piece about it here.

Some time before 1900 a shrewd lawyer (or lawyers) for one of the big coal or steel companies drafted a form for the conveyance of mineral rights. It came to be called a "broad form" deed because it contained a comprehensive enumeration of the rights and privileges that were included along with the ownership of the minerals themselves. It explicitly specified the right to use the surface of the land "in any and every manner that may be deemed necessary or convenient for mining" and contained a waiver of any resulting damages. At that time there were no railroads into the coal-rich areas of eastern Kentucky and, needless to say, the very notion of strip-mining was several generations yet to come. Coal rights in that country had little or no current value because there was no economical way to get the coal out. It had real value only to corporate speculators who could buy and hold it into the future, as in the instance of Florida real estate back in that day and time.

Along came a bright and well-educated young man named John C. C. Mayo, born and raised in that part of the state. Having thoroughly schooled himself on the geology of eastern Kentucky, he knew that the coal was there and he had the foresight to realize that the big northern industrialists would be interested in acquiring it for future development. He knew also that because it did not yet have any real value the owners of the land would be glad to take whatever they could get for it. So he took a trip up north and arranged with one of those companies for the necessary financing to purchase options and then conveyances of the coal rights. The broad form deed was used for the conveyances, and though others eventually copied it, it was and is commonly referred to as the Mayo broad form deed. John Mayo became quite wealthy, and a real magnate in the world of coal mining. He built a fine mansion in Paintsville and lived there until he died. I have read that when his funeral was held in 1914 there were more private railroad cars in Paintsville than could have been found anywhere else in the country.

In later years, by reason of the extensive rights conferred on the mineral owners under these deeds our courts referred to them as the "dominant" owners of the land:

"The mineral estate under the deed is dominant, superior, and exclusive in every circumstance or condition where the owner thereof shall deem it necessary or convenient to make use of the surface as the deed allows." *McIntire v. Marian Coal Company,* 190 Ky. 342, 227 S.W. 298, 300 (1921).

In the course of the litigation over the broad form deed it was argued that if it really had been intended for the mineral owners to have the untrammeled right to do as they saw fit with the surface of the land they surely would have bought the whole thing, surface, minerals and all. However, under the law (of Kentucky at least), when the title to a mineral has been severed from the surface title, the adverse possession of a squatter on the surface cannot ripen into ownership of the previously severed minerals. Whether that principle actually figured into the original drafting of the broad form deed I do not know, and I doubt whether anybody knows, but it certainly provides a good reason for not acquiring the entire title. Another more plausible explanation might be that the mineral owners probably were not eager to pay taxes on the largely timbered surface, which at that stage of history had more value than the minerals.

During Mr. Mayo's trips into the hills it was his custom to carry a bag of gold coins and to give one of the gold pieces to the lady of the house whenever he closed a deal for the minerals. My old friend John Calhoun Wells, former Secretary of the Kentucky Labor Cabinet, and a native of Auxier, a coal-mining town near Prestonsburg, told me that during these trips his father used to accompany Mr. Mayo as his bodyguard.

In the 1921 *McIntire* case the court said that the mineral owner could destroy the crops and buildings on the surface, but would have to pay for the damage. In later years the court overruled that portion of the opinion requiring the mineral owner to pay for surface damages, reasoning that if one has a legal right to do something it is illogical to require him to pay for doing it. See *Martin v. Kentucky Oak Mining Company*, Ky., 429 S.W.2d 395, 399 (1968).

The first case in which the court was called on to decide whether a mineral owner had the right to strip-mine without express authorization in his deed was *Treadway v. Wilson*, 310 Ky. 702, 192 S.W.2d 949 (1946), from Clay County, involving a 1907 conveyance that was *not* a broad form deed. In determining that the mineral owner did have the right to strip-mine, the court quoted from an earlier opinion [*Case v. Elkhorn Coal Co.*, 210 Ky. 700, 276 S.W. 573, 574 (1925)] to the effect that the mineral owner has the "paramount right to the use of the surface in the prosecution of its business for any purpose of necessity or convenience, and of this it is to be the judge, unless it exercises this power oppressively, arbitrarily, wantonly, or maliciously." However, as the surface owner in this instance was claiming that the mineral owner's use of the proposed surface-mining technique would in fact be oppressive, the case was returned to the trial court for the purpose of having that factual issue decided. After a hearing, the trial court found that the coal in question could not be successfully removed by any method other than stripping and that the mineral owner was entitled to recover it in that manner. There was no appeal from this final result.

As I remember it, the big earth-moving machines did not begin to flood the country until after World War II, and of course strip-mining on a large scale came along with those machines. Thus *Treadway* appears to have been the opening gun that culminated in the 30-year assault on the broad form deed. Real hostilities, though, began 10 years later, with *Buchanan v. Watson,* Ky., 290 S.W.2d 40 (1956), which involved a classic 1903 broad form conveyance of mineral rights in Magoffin County to John C. C. Mayo. The case presented two questions – whether the mineral owner could remove the coal by a strip-mining process that would destroy the surface owned by another, and, if so, would the coal owner be liable to the surface owner for the resulting damages to the surface?

As sometimes happens when the losing party files a petition for rehearing, there were two opinions in this case. The first, written by Commissioner Watson Clay, affirmed the judgment of the trial court (John Chris Cornett), answering both questions in the affirmative. After rehearing, however, this opinion was withdrawn and replaced by a new opinion, written by Judge Montgomery, reversing that part of the trial judgment declaring that the surface owner could recover for damage to the surface. Oddly, this opinion quotes from the *McIntire* case but does not make any reference to its qualification that if the taking destroys or renders useless any improvements on the surface, including the "residence, barn, garden, orchard, well," etc., the owner must be compensated (227 S.W. at p. 300). As it happened, the case did not involve any such improvements, but on its face it does stand for the flat proposition that under a broad form deed the mineral owner may do whatever is reasonably necessary in order to recover the minerals and is not liable for damage thereby occasioned to the surface.

In retrospect, the owners of mineral rights under broad form deeds probably would have been better off had the court held fast to its first opinion. As it is, *Buchanan* became the evil villain against which the press, public, and a host of landowners in eastern Kentucky raised and carried on the tide of opposition that eventually engulfed the broad form deed and divested the mineral owners of their judicially-declared right to strip or auger mine.

The issues in *Buchanan* were clear and the decision was clear. The opinion was unanimous. It should have ended the controversy. But it didn't. Over the next 12 years the same question was brought to the court six more times, and in each instance the court reiterated what it had held before, and in each case the decision was again unanimous. Those cases were:

Bevander Coal Company v. Matney, Ky., 320 S.W.2d 301 (1959).

Blue Diamond Coal Company v. Neace, Ky., 337 S.W.2d 725 (1960), in which it was pointed out that *Buchanan* did not upset any existing law, but had merely applied old principles to a new fact situation. This was my introduction to the broad form deed. Judge Montgomery, author of the *Buchanan* opinion, was then the Chief Justice, and he assigned the case to me and advised me in the preparation of my opinion. This case did involve damage to the improvements (and timber), which according to the 1921 *McIntire* opinion would have entitled the surface owner to compensation, but I was under the impression that *Buchanan* had overruled it. Evidently Montgomery and the rest of the court thought so too. In later years Judge Stephenson wrote a concurring opinion in another case [*Kentland-Elkhorn Coal Company v. Charles*, Ky., 514 S.W.2d 659, 664 (1974)] pointing out this discrepancy, but from a jurisprudential standpoint at least it really amounts to no more than a technicality (in that the defunct status of the *McIntire* language was not specifically made official in *Blue Diamond*), because that result certainly was the intent of the court and was in fact expressed in later cases, such as *Martin* (429 S.W.2d 395, 399).

Kodak Coal Company v. Smith, Ky., 338 S.W.2d 699 (1960).

Ritchie v. Midland Mining Company, Ky., 347 S.W.2d 548 (1961).

Blue Diamond Coal Company v. Campbell, Ky., 371 S.W.2d 483(1963).

Croley v. Round Mountain Coal Company, Ky., 374 S.W.2d 852 (1964). The deed in this case was not the traditional

"Mayo" form, but the court held that if the coal cannot be removed in any other way it can be stripped or auger-mined. A further difference from the earlier cases was that in this instance the deed severing the mineral rights had been made in 1948, at a time when the parties must have been aware of the existence of strip-mining.

At the time of the *Buchanan* case (1956) the member of the court from the coal-mining area of eastern Kentucky was Astor Hogg, who was defeated by Robert Bird in the 1956 Eisenhower landslide. Judge Bird joined in all of the broad form deed decisions until he was succeeded by Edward P. Hill, of Prestonsburg, in 1965.

The next major battle in the broad form deed war came with *Martin v. Kentucky Oak Mining Company,* Ky., 429 S.W.2d 395 (1968), from Knott County, and it was at this point that the solidarity of the court on that issue began to unravel. Meanwhile, several years earlier it had decided an oil and gas case from Magoffin County, *Wiser Oil Company v. Conley,* Ky., 346 S.W.2d 718 (1960), in which it denied the claimed right of the mineral owners to waterflood the premises in order to effect a secondary recovery of oil. Although the mineral deed contained provisions allowing for the use of the surface, it was not a broad form deed, and the court held that *Buchanan* was not applicable. I mention the *Wiser* opinion here because later on it was strongly argued that it was inconsistent with *Buchanan.* (If so, perhaps it was *Wiser* that was wrong.) Anyway, in a quite comprehensive opinion written by Commissioner Robert Cullen the court again stood by the *Buchanan* line of cases, but for the first time there was a dissent. Earl Osborne (who had succeeded Brady Stewart) dissented on the technical ground that he thought we should not have taken the case, but Judge Hill, in a colorful opinion that earned him a degree of fame, dissented on the merits – charging, among other things, that "*Wiser* and *Buchanan* are as inconsistent as sin and salvation."

At this point Jim Milliken, who had been one of the members of the court when it unanimously decided *Buchanan*, and had joined without a sigh of disapproval in all of the other cases which had followed it thereafter, decided to jump ship, and added his name to Hill's dissenting opinion. By this time, of course, the press had gotten into the act (who can forget that newsphoto of the "widder Combs" threatening to throw herself under a bulldozer?), and there had been some uncomplimentary remarks directed at the court. I recall, for example, its having been said or suggested that we were beholden to the coal industry, which was not true. Whether this kind of stuff affected Milliken I do not know and would not guess. But anyway, he was a gentle, tender-hearted man with a frustrating (to the rest of us) tendency to sway back and forth on a question from one day to the next.

For some unaccountable reason Milliken was back in the fold when the next broad form deed case arose. This was *Rice v. Stapleton,* Ky., 502 S.W.2d 522 (1973), from Johnson County. By this time Hill had left the court and had been succeeded by James B. Stephenson, of Pikeville, who in his previous capacity as a circuit judge had been the trial judge and therefore did not participate in our consideration of the case. The mineral severance in question was a 1903 deed to John Mayo. At the trial stage the surface owner recovered $3,000 for damage to the surface. The court held that in the absence of a showing of an arbitrary, wanton or malicious exercise of its rights the mineral owner should have been given a directed verdict. Pleas Jones, of Williamsburg, who had come onto the court since the time of the Martin opinion, dissented without comment, and Scott Reed, of Lexington, who also had not been a member of the court when it had a broad form deed case before it, concurred in the result only, without explanatory comment. The author of the court's opinion was Commissioner Roy Vance, of Paducah, later to be one of the elected members of the court.

The next move was a 1974 act of the legislature requiring the holder of mineral rights under a broad form deed to obtain the surface owner's written consent in order to get a permit to strip-mine. C. 350, Acts of 1974. This, of course, was an attempted diminution of the rights theretofore held to be vested in the mineral owner, and in a unanimous opinion written by Robert Lukowsky the court held it unconstitutional. *Department for Nat. R. & E. Pro. v. No. 8 Ltd. of Va.,* Ky., 528 S.W.2d 684 (1975). There is no indication that either of the two justices from eastern Kentucky then sitting (Jones and Stephenson) had any quarrel with or criticism of this decision. In a later opinion, discussed below, Stephenson brushed it off as irrelevant for the reason that in his opinion its "simple holding" was merely that the statute was an impermissible exercise of the police power (!). (To the contrary, however, see *Akers v. Baldwin*, Ky., 736 S.W.2d at p. 315, in which at p. 310 the majority opinion of Chief Justice Stephens correctly cites it for the specific proposition that a "statute that functions retroactively to determine the meaning of a preexisting deed is constitutionally impermissible because it impairs the obligation of a contract.")

In *Commerce Union Bank v. Kinkade,* Ky., 540 S.W.2d 861 (1976), from Muhlenberg County, in western Kentucky, it was decided that the rights granted under several mineral deeds were not as broad as those enumerated in broad form deeds and did not include the right to strip-mine. Four of the members of the court (Clayton, Lukowsky, Palmore and Sternberg) concurred in a *per curiam* opinion, and the other three in separate opinions. Stephenson delivered up an extensive essay criticizing almost all the court had said and done through all the years from *Treadway* on and leaving with the conclusion that all of it should be overruled. Jones joined in this opinion without separate comment. Chief Justice Reed concurred with a brief opinion saying that although he agreed with Stephenson, he "could not . . . destroy the property rights of parties who entered into voluntary relationships in the light of plainly expressed existing law" (540 S.W.2d at pp. 869, 870).

The year 1982 saw the election of four new judges to the Supreme Court. Clayton was defeated by Roy Vance, of Paducah, a highly competent member of the Court of Appeals who had been one of the commissioners of our court before the Judicial Amendment of 1975. Jay O'Hara, of Covington, who had served for a short time following the untimely death of the intellectually gifted Robert Lukowsky, was defeated by Donald Wintersheimer. Charles Leibson, a brilliant trial lawyer from Louisville, succeeded Marvin Sternberg, and William Gant, of Owensboro, another member of the Court of Appeals, succeeded me. Scott Reed had already left to become a federal judge and was succeeded by Robert Stephens, who followed me as Chief Justice.

In the fall of 1980 I had taken part in the midyear meeting of the Kentucky Bar Association, which consisted of a Caribbean cruise.

During this time I became acquainted with Bruce Stephens, of Hazard, a fine lawyer and officer of the Kentucky River Coal Company, who had successfully practiced the *Buchanan* case in 1956. During a deck-chair conversation with him I remember suggesting that it might be better for the coal people if there were not any more broad form deed cases. Some day they might lose one. At this time, with my term of office drawing to a close, it did not occur to me that I might later be personally involved as a lawyer. Little did I know!

Several years later, after I had returned to the practice of law in Henderson, I received a telephone call from Bill Caylor, of the Kentucky Coal Association, asking if I could come to Lexington and meet with a group of coal representatives to discuss some litigation. The upshot of this meeting was that I agreed to represent five owners of coal properties whose title derived from broad form deeds and who wished to challenge the validity of H.B. 32, a 1984 act of the legislature providing that in the absence of clear and convincing evidence to the contrary the parties to any mineral-severance deed *theretofore or thereafter* executed must be held to have intended that the coal be extracted only by the method or methods of commercial coal extraction commonly known to be in use in the area at the time the instrument was executed. This, of course, would have destroyed the right of mineral owners derived from broad form deeds to surface-mine without the surface-owners' consent, and for more reasons than one was grossly unconstitutional, as the court soon thereafter held in *Akers v. Baldwin*, Ky., 736 S.W.2d 294 (1987). In so holding, however, being mindful, no doubt, of the relentless clamor of the opposition environmentalists and their media supporters, the court narrowed the *Buchanan* rule by holding that henceforth, except for "all conveyances by broad form deed, and leases and mining efforts under broad form deeds, made between the effective date of *Buchanan*, May 4, 1956, and the initial rendition date of this decision July 2, 1987. . . . whenever the mineral rights under a broad form deed include the right to use the entire surface to extract the minerals, the mineral owner may do so, but must respond to the surface owner for all damages to that estate," etc. (736 S.W.2d at p. 307.)

This decision spawned four separate opinions, one by Chief

Justice Stephens (the prevailing opinion), joined by Justices Leibson and Gant, a concurring opinion by Justice Vance, joined also by Gant, and opinions by Stephenson and Lambert concurring in part and dissenting in part, with Wintersheimer joining in both. Four of these judges, Gant, Leibson, Lambert and Wintersheimer, were of course new to the court since the last broad form deed case. The two judges from eastern Kentucky, Stephenson and Lambert, saw no constitutional problem with HB 32 and would completely overrule *Buchanan* anyway. Wintersheimer joined in their essentially dissenting opinions. Again, as in *Commerce Union,* Stephenson disgorged another carping farrago, suggesting this time that those of us who had been following *Buchanan* must not have read it, and that the Chief Justice's majority opinion displayed "a fundamental misunderstanding" of many of the opinions it had cited. (By this time, of course, all but one of those poor illiterates had either died or retired from the court.)

For whatever academic interest it may have, one of the principal arguments made in *Akers* was that the doctrine of separation of powers prohibits the legislature from undertaking to determine the legal effect of past transactions. *Akers* held specifically that in enacting this statute the legislature had exceeded the bounds of its constitutional authority, which alone was sufficient to invalidate it. Incredibly, none of the dissenters attempted even to address this dispositive point.

The effect of *Akers* was to protect only "the property rights of parties who [had] entered into voluntary relationships in the light of plainly expressed existing law," as so well put by Scott Reed in his opinion concurring with the result in *Commerce Union.* Unfortunately, however, it would appear that the broad form deed, as the court had construed it, had done its work. It was not enough to say "no more." Those rights, constitutional or not, simply had to be extinguished – retroactively. Public pressure, aroused, stimulated and fanned by the press, brought forth a constitutional amendment consisting essentially of the same statutory provisions that had been held invalid in *Akers.*

It was my opinion, and still is, that this amendment of the state constitution would not stand muster under the federal constitution. There were and are respectable authorities to support the argument that it effected a taking of property without compensation and without due process of law and impaired the obligation of contracts. In due course a suit was brought in the Franklin Circuit Court to enjoin its being submitted to a public vote. In this action it was alleged that the plaintiffs and their predecessors in interest had acquired their coal rights under broad form deeds in reliance upon the decisions of our court holding that such conveyances included the right to recover the coal by surface mining, and that in their cases the coal could not be economically recovered in any other way. These allegations were supported in the form of affidavits filed with a motion for summary judgment. Procedurally, if there is no honest denial of the facts, presented by affidavit, that would entitle the moving party to a judgment, he should have it without further litigational rigmarole. Unfortunately, however, perhaps because in Kentucky our judges are elected and are naturally reluctant to incur the displeasure of their lawyers, this quick, fair and clear way of resolving a controversy has never been very popular. In this particular case, which I practiced for the plaintiffs, it was vital that we have a judgment as far in advance of the election as possible, but it was equally to the advantage of the Attorney General to delay things, so we did not get any cooperation from him, and finally, on the eve of the election, the trial judge declined to give us a summary, so I dismissed the action, which would have become moot after the election. Considering the general unpopularity of our cause, I certainly understand that it would have required a judge of extraordinary backbone to stop the election, but it does seem ironic that both he and the Attorney General had ambitions to run for the office of Lieutenant Governor at the next general election. (Both ran, and both were defeated.) The amendment passed, of course, by a huge majority.

Meanwhile, another broad form deed suit had erupted in Johnson County. Not surprisingly, the surface owners had prevailed in the trial court, but lost in the Court of Appeals and appealed that decision to the Kentucky Supreme Court. At this time I was practicing law with the firm of Jackson & Kelly in Lexington, and J. K. Wells, the attorney in Paintsville who represented the coal owners, asked us to help him in the Supreme Court, with the result that I wrote the brief and argued the case in that court. Here again arises an amazing story.

On June 30, 1993, while the matter was pending in the Supreme Court, Dan Jack Combs, one of its members, resigned his office. Then on July 13 the court entered an order appointing the same Combs to succeed himself until such time as the court's decision in this particular case (not yet rendered) should become final. Two days later the governor appointed Sara Combs (widow of Bert Combs) to fill the vacancy created by Dan Jack's resignation, and on the same day the court issued a 4 to 3 decision reversing the Court of Appeals and reinstating the judgment of the trial court. Dan Jack, of course, was one of the four majority votes. I have no reason to believe, and do not believe, that Sara had anything to do with, or even was aware of, this incredible turn of events. Whether she or Dan Jack (or both) participated in the subsequent denial of our petition for rehearing I do not know, but so far as I know the order appointing Dan Jack to serve until the rendition of a final decision was never revoked or modified. All of this irregularity was called to the attention of the court in our petition for rehearing, but was ignored without comment.

The majority opinion upholding the constitutional amendment, *Ward v. Harding,* Ky., 860 S.W.2d 280 (1993), was written by Justice Lambert, who was joined by Justices Wintersheimer, Spain, and Dan Jack Combs. This was about as expected except for Spain, who was from the coal area of Western Kentucky and should have had a better knowledge of mineral law than some of the others. Strip-mining is an ugly business, however, and it may be that having seen so much of it in his own back yard he had developed an undisclosed aversion to it. On the other hand, I have always detested it myself, but I suppose I am too much of an old-fashioned lawyer to let my personal attitude toward it to override my duty as a judge. Anyway, Tom Spain is a fine man and an old friend – I am just voicing my lamentation.

I hope the reader is not growing weary of this story, because there is a little more yet to be said.

It is pretty well beyond cavil that a legislative body cannot constitutionally enact a law retroactively changing property rights, as our legislature sought to do in 1984 with H.B. 32. By parity of reasoning, the same constitutional principle applies to the courts. A state supreme court has no more right to authorize an unconstitutional violation of property rights than the legislature does. "The federal guaranty of due process extends to state action through its judicial as well as through its legislative, executive, or administrative branch of government." *Brinkerhoff-Faris Trust & Savings Co. v. Hill*, 281 U.S. 673, 680 (1930). "For a state cannot be permitted to defeat the constitutional prohibition against taking property without due process of law by the simple device of asserting retroactively that the property it has taken never existed at all." Stewart, J., concurring in *Hughes v. State of Washington,* 389 U.S. 290, 298 (1967). Yet this is the very thing that took place in *Ward v. Harding*. The court simply overruled the entire line of decisions to the contrary, disregarding the fact that people had bought their rights in reliance upon those decisions, and then said that because the decisions were now being retroactively overruled, such rights never existed in the first place and thus could not have been violated. (!!)

For those who may be sufficiently interested in this particular subject I recommend a reading of the dissenting opinion issued by the late Charles Leibson, surely one of the very finest lawyers ever to sit on our court, which appears at 860 S.W.2d 289.

Our only recourse from this atrocious decision was to apply for a writ of certiorari from the United States Supreme Court, but this proved to be of no avail, despite the efforts of a fine law firm in Washington, D.C. They were convinced that our position was correct and they could win the case if the court would hear it, but it is not easy to catch the ear of the U.S. Supreme Court with a mundane question of property rights, and this would be especially so if it is being asked to tell a state supreme court that it, the court itself, has violated the Constitution. It must be recognized too that the U.S. Supreme Court receives thousands of petitions for certiorari every year, which means that the drudgery of winnowing through them falls to the their corps of law clerks. And no matter how smart and well-educated fresh young law graduates may be, they are not likely to exercise the judgment that might be expected of the justices themselves. Certainly none of the justices has the time to look in depth at all those petitions, so the choice of which ones they do take must necessarily be influenced by what these clerks recommend.

As of this writing no federal court has decided or been asked to decide whether the Kentucky amendment violates the federal constitution. It is still an open question, but as time passes and the competing interests have made adjustments according to their individual circumstances it will be more and more difficult to get any court to upset the boat again. But a great injustice has been done to many people in the coal business whose only fault was to rely on what the highest court in this state for the better part of a century said was the law.

One of the regrets I have about the broad form deed controversy is that I seem to have fallen from grace with the *Courier-Journal,* the newspaper I had read and trusted for most of my life. As a matter of fact, I carried the paper for a couple of years while I was a boy in Bowling Green. Not that I was the best or most dedicated newsboy in town, but somehow I have always had a little sense of pride in having delivered papers for the *C-J* and, before that, for the old *Bowling Green Times-Journal,* published by a splendid old gentleman named Jesse Denhardt. Anyway, during my years on the court I always felt – with dubious justification, I suppose – that my work had the approval of the paper. Be that as it may, after I left the court, and when I was employed as a practicing lawyer to defend a group of coal companies, things began to sour. Once during the early '70's I had been with a hunting party in Ballard County that included Barry Bingham, Jr. (before the days of the long-handled mustachio), and we had mildly crossed swords at the breakfast table over the broad form deed issue. We later exchanged letters on the subject, and as I recall it now (I do not have a copy of the letter before me) I asked him why, if the paper was so much against strip-mining, they didn't encourage an effort to have it outlawed. But no, they wouldn't go that far.

I have always suspected that the Binghams (especially Barry's mother, a great lady for whom I had the utmost admiration) gave some encouragement and probably financial backing to the lawyers who were practicing the litigation for the people who were seeking to change the law (without the benefit of clergy, as they used to say about common-law marriages). It appeared to me that nearly every time one of those cases was about to come up for decision by our court an editorial or special article favoring that side of the case would appear in the paper. This sort of indirect communication, or attempted communication, to the judge or judges of a court by persons other than the lawyers who have been retained by the parties to make their arguments for them, is a practice I always thought to be underhanded, regardless of what the supercilious news media may perceive as their proper function in life. And in this particular instance it is difficult for me to understand how newspaper editors and others who are educated and otherwise intelligent people can have so little regard for fundamental constitutional principles such as the right not to have one's property taken or destroyed without just compensation.

It seems to me that two major factors produced the broad form deed controversy. The first was a lack of understanding. It never occurred to the average person who bought the surface rights to a piece of property that he was not the real owner of the property. Even today it is not easy for some people to comprehend the theory of split titles. If you own the surface and can build a house on it, the land is yours. Manifestly, there were many who bought property without having the title examined, and there must have been numerous instances in which the title examiner did not explain the implications of the mineral title under a broad form deed. Yet there it was all the time – at least as far back as 1921, when the court in *McIntire v. Marian Coal Company* plainly said that the mineral estate was "dominant, superior, and exclusive." And of course the mineral deed itself – the broad form deed – could scarcely have said it any louder. The surface owner could have only what the mineral owner did not now or in the distant future need or want. Had this been explained to (and understood by) the prospective buyer of the surface, he would not have taken the property. But obviously they did not understand it.

The second factor was the unanticipated advent of heavy earth-moving equipment and its consequent strip-mining. Sinking shafts, laying a few roads and tracks, building tipples and creating slag heaps were bad enough, but the complete destruction of the surface was unthinkable. Yet the plain meaning of the mineral deed was that they could do it, and when they did, it hit the fan.

This is what happened, as I see it. The surface owners never realized or understood how much their predecessors in title had sold off to the mineral owner. Then the strip-mining era came along and they found out. The time was ripe for bleeding hearts, and they rose to the occasion – legal principles be damned.

When I was practicing law in Henderson long years ago we had lots of mineral litigation, usually involving oil and gas rights. Many times a property owner made a little money by selling off the coal rights, oil and gas rights, or both. There had been much coal mining long before they struck oil in that part of the state. In time the courts decided that if the "coal and mineral" rights had been sold off or reserved, those rights included oil, because oil is a mineral. But, cried the surface owner, back when that deed was made nobody knew about oil, and they didn't mean oil. No matter, said the courts, whether you ever heard of it or not, or what you might have done if you had known it, oil is a mineral, and the deed said minerals, so that's it. In another case in a different part of Kentucky, on the same principle, the court held that the word "minerals" in a deed included diamonds, regardless of whether diamonds in the ground had ever been heard of in this part of the world. In other words, it has been a firmly established principle that a written instrument must be taken to mean what it says, notwithstanding what either or both of the parties to it contemplated or thought it meant. That is the principle that has been violated in the broad form deed proceedings.

From the standpoint of pure jurisprudence, I think, the lesson of the broad form deed cases is that when the hoofbeats of public opinion get loud enough logic will become irrelevant and the law will be twisted into another shape by the courts themselves. Perhaps this fact of life ought not be too greatly decried, however, because after all, survival is the first law of nature, and as the great Holmes said and the long history of the common law has amply demonstrated, in a free society the survival of law depends on the satisfaction of its customers, the people. And the public is often too impatient to brook the law's delays. So it happens that every now and then the judges (especially if they are elected by popular vote) will find a short-cut that suits the public taste.

Bernard Davis used to say that sometimes when a court has a

difficult time deciding a case the way it would like to have it decided, it might have to use a law wrench, or even a fact wrench. To illustrate, a cynic might suggest that in the 2003 primary election contest in which the court ruled that it was not fatal for a gubernatorial candidate to be without a qualified running mate at the expiration of the time for filing, the court may very well have used its law wrench. Certainly it would have looked bad to tell the people they could not vote for one of the leading candidates. And even judges don't like to look bad. (Incidentally, there are plenty of lawyers, whether cynics or not, who would say that the poor old 1891 Constitution was stretched plumb out of its skin in the famous *Toyota* case. But I guess we needed the jobs more than we need the law.)

CHAPTER 4
FURTHER REFLECTIONS ON JURISPRUDENCE

It has been said that the law is not what is written in the books but what the judges say it is. A crude way to put it, but it happens to be the truth. Judge-made law originated in England long before Simon de Montfort convened the first legislative body comprised of common citizens, and it has been the life blood of a common-law system which over the course of more than eight centuries developed most of the body of law existing in America today. Originally, when a court of last resort decided not to follow an existing judicial precedent, it simply declared that the precedent was mistaken and thus it really never was the law in the first place. (Shades of the broad form deed case!) Eventually, however, overruling a precedent did not carry with it a cancellation of all that had been said and done in reliance upon it. The point to be recognized here is that the whole history of the common law consisted of a series of decisions in which the courts in effect disregarded the laws of yesterday by simply overruling them and substituting their own ideas of what the judges thought the law ought to be in their own time. That is how the law grew and, as Jefferson might have put it, the coat that fitted the boy of yesterday was altered to fit the man of today.

Having undertaken to discuss (not, I hope, *ad nauseam*) the slippery subject of jurisprudence, I feel obligated to end it with a *caveat.* When I first became a judge I had read a good deal about it and had developed much the same philosophy that I still hold today. However, at that time some of the more conservative members of the bar – prisoners still of *stare decisis* – beheld me as something of a radical. You will recall, for example, my having mentioned Mr. Caldwell, of Ashland, who, according to Bert Combs, was under the mistaken impression that I thought the courts could and should make and unmake the law from day to day, more or less at will. And unfortunately, the 40 years or so since then have seen a decided tilt in that direction. So I want to make it crystal clear that while I do not believe precedents ought to be applied like a slide rule, they should not be overturned unless they clearly were wrong in the first place or unless they are no longer consistent with the settled attitudes and conditions of life now prevailing. As the great Holmes said, the life of the law has not been logic, but experience. Logic without vision is a suicidal trap. But this does not mean that judges have a right to twist the law to suit what they as individuals think it ought to be – that is, because they don't like it. And certainly trial judges have no authority whatever in this area.

An early example in my career will serve as an appropriate conclusion. When I was a senior in law school I was one of the contestants in the final moot court competition. The question of the debate was whether the Roosevelt administration's recently-enacted Fair Labor Standards Act was constitutional. I had been raised in a rock-ribbed Republican family and, at that point in my salad days, had no use for Roosevelt or for labor unions. (Don't shoot! I have long since changed my mind.) Ironically, my side of the argument was to defend the Act. Our biggest obstacle was a case named *Hammer v. Dagenhart,* in which the U. S. Supreme Court had decided some 20 years before that a piece of legislation outlawing child labor was unconstitutional. So this was my first experience in arguing that a perfectly valid precedent should be overruled. We won the case (among our three judges were the late Churchill Humphrey, of the Jefferson Circuit Court, and James Stites, of the Kentucky Court of Appeals, both brilliant lawyers in every sense of the word), and not long thereafter the Supreme Court itself did overrule *Hammer v. Dagenhart* and upheld the Fair Labor Standards Act. Now, what I am seeking to illustrate is that here was a precedent that may or may not have been right when it was decided, but right or wrong, it certainly was no longer right for the world of today. This is the kind of situation in which a court is justified in castrating a precedent.

CHAPTER 5
ACAPULCO AND PERCY FOREMAN

One of the memorable experiences of my time on the court was a visit to Acapulco, Mexico, in the 1960's, during the Nixon presidency. One day while I was working in my office at Room 201 in the state capitol the telephone rang, and it was Frank Haddad and Rush Nicholson, calling from Louisville. Both of these gentlemen practiced in the field of criminal law (Frank probably was the best known criminal lawyer in Kentucky at the time) and one of them was currently president of the National Association of Trial Lawyers in Criminal Cases. It was just a week or two before the annual convention of that organization, which was to be held in Acapulco. Nixon's attorney general, John Mitchell, was scheduled to be the speaker at their annual banquet. However, he suddenly canceled the engagement, and my two friends were desperate to find a substitute speaker.

Apparently they had about scraped the bottom of the barrel, so they asked me if I would do it. I had never been to Mexico, so I was really pleased to go, provided that I could take my wife, Eleanor, with me. They readily agreed to this condition, and we went to Acapulco.

There was a wonderful old lodging complex – too nice, I think, to be called a motel – called the Las Brisas, on a high hill south of the town overlooking the Pacific Ocean bay. A pink Jeep was loaned to each patron so he could get up and down the hill and get around town. Every room had its own little private swimming pool, and a continental-type breakfast was delivered to the door every morning. Talk about luxury! Everything but a personal servant.

The lawyers and their wives were an extremely attractive and convivial group of people. Melvin Belli, who at that time was at the zenith of his fabulous career, did not attend, but most everybody knew him, and he frequently came up in the conversation. I remember, for example, that the lawyers referred to him at "Fatso," though I did not have the impression that he was a fat man. But the equally notable Percy Foreman, likewise at the peak of his own career, was there with his wife and daughter, and we all enjoyed them. Percy's wife was a lovely lady who had started out as a ballet dancer, and they called their little girl "Sputnik" because she had come into the world at the same time as the Russian space craft of that name had made its successful flight into the stratosphere.

Percy was a great big, friendly man with an infectious personality. He had been consulted in the notorious Jack Ruby case, but had not accepted employment in it. At the time, he was involved in a big civil controversy in Florida over some woman's entitlement (or non-entitlement) to a fabulous collection of jewelry. We all kidded him about his fee, though he never told us what it was, or might be.

For the banquet I wore a white suit and a black string tie and, with my head of white hair, I told the crowd that I wanted them to see what Col. Sanders would look like without his beard. I did not attempt to make a serious speech – after all, with so many gregarious people, away from home, in a festive humor and well fortified with liquid refreshments, who wants to hear a sober speech? I just told a few funny stories and all went well. Percy got a bang out of my revealing what I thought was his secret fee schedule – "all you've got."

I had known Rush Nicholson for many years. He grew up in Buechel, a suburb of Louisville on the Bardstown Road, where his mother operated a popular home-style restaurant in her home. When I entered the University of Louisville law school in the fall of 1936 Nick was one of my classmates. He did not do so well the first semester, and was on his way to Florida to take up some other occupation when he stopped in Lebanon, Tennessee, to see a friend who was a student at Cumberland Law School. The friend persuaded him to enroll at Cumberland, which he did. In those days it was permissible to take the Kentucky bar examination after two years in law school, which most of us did, so I passed the bar in 1938, a year before I graduated from law school in June of 1939. The point of this story is that Rush Nicholson, who started out in my class but dropped out, nevertheless took the bar exam and passed it at the same time as I did, in 1938. Later on he became one of the judges of the Jefferson Circuit Court, and his son, Jimmy, is a long-time district judge in Louisville.

Nick and his wife, Sarah, are both gone now. At Acapulco their daughter was still at teenager, and she was very much the life of the party. We had a great time together. Memories, memories.

CHAPTER 6
OLD MEMORIES

The toughest part of writing a narrative like this is in bringing it to a close. As of now, it has been over 20 years since my departure from the court, and although I have never really missed it I have fond memories of the lawyers and judges and of the people who worked for the court while I was there, and I want to mention some of them here. Also, running for and serving on the court quite naturally brought me into a new world, and occasioned many unforgettable events with old and new friends.

One of the joys of being a lawyer is that you get to know so many real characters. From law school on it has been one of the great privileges of my life to know and associate with so many colorful individuals – unfortunately, however, too many to dwell upon within a legitimate scope for this commentary on my time as a judge.

J. R. Miller

My story would not be complete without further mention of J. R. Miller, whose help was so great and so vital in the 1959 election. I first met J. R. when I was a young lawyer practicing in Henderson. He came to my office one day and asked me if I would help in a money-raising effort for the Boy Scouts. I never had the privilege of being a Scout during my boyhood, but I liked this man at once, and I readily agreed to do what I could. This proved to be the beginning of one of the best friendships of my life. J. R. was the manager of the RECC operation in Owensboro and a stout friend of Earle Clements. He was vigorously involved in politics and was one of my first allies in Owensboro. Daviess and Warren were the most heavily populated counties in the Second District, so of course in my race for the court Owensboro was of the utmost importance. Dan Griffith, a popular lawyer, was at that time the Commonwealth's Attorney in Owensboro, and his friends were encouraging him to make the race. However, when he contacted Doc Beauchamp to see if he could get his support Doc told him that he was already for me, and that was that. Doc, of course, also was a stout Clements man, and was my great and good friend for the rest of his life. It was his steadfast loyalty that discouraged anyone else from taking me on in the reelection years of 1966 and 1974.

Anyway, and happily for all, the movers and shakers of political affairs in Owensboro, including a rising young star named Wendell Ford, managed to arrange for Dan Griffith to succeed Judge Sid Neal as judge of the Daviess Circuit Court, and largely by reason of their cooperation and the efforts of J. R., when the results came in from Daviess County on election night I knew it was all over. I had carried 14 of the 16 counties from my district, including Daviess, Henderson, and Warren in the Democratic primary and all 16 in the Republican primary.

J. R. was a native of Vicksburg, Mississippi, and some time after I had become a member of the court – probably in 1960 – he invited me and my close friend Fred Vogel, former county judge of

Henderson County, to fly down there in the RECC airplane and go fishing for a couple of days at Eagle Lake, a Mississippi River cut-off some 10 miles north of Vicksburg. J. R. had two brothers, Don and Louis, who lived at Vicksburg, and one (or both) of them either owned or had access to a little lodge by the lakeside, so that was our headquarters. One night J. R.'s brothers put on a cookout for us, and we had a great feed by the fireside, followed by a crap game in which I seem to recall that Louis was the big winner and J. R. lost several hundred dollars. (I did not participate in the game.) Anyway, to get to the point of this story, one of the guests at this party was an elderly gentleman named Simrall, whose son, Newell, was a boyhood friend of J. R.'s but was out of town and could not be there. As we sat around the fire Mr. Simrall regaled us with some of his reminiscences of old times and places, one of which was that when he was a teen-age boy he and a friend had gone to the World's Fair in St. Louis and, while there, had sneaked into a whorehouse. I can see him now, with a gentle, shy little grin, as he said, "Boys, that was the first time I ever knew white women did that."

If I ever heard a story that told more than that one, I don't remember it. Old Mississippi! I have often wished I could pass this story on to Shelby Foote – I believe he would get a kick out of it.

Some years after our trip to Mississippi J. R. was elected Mayor of Owensboro, and then a boulevard was named after him. At the time he ran for Mayor there was a statute requiring that a candidate for Mayor be a resident for a certain number of years, and there was a question as to whether J. R. was eligible to run, as he had lived for some time just outside the city limits of Owensboro. Several of his friends among the prominent lawyers in town concluded that he could not run. However, there was a green young lawyer named Carol Pate in Bill Rummage's law office who thought she remembered a fairly recent series of cases in which similar statutes had been held invalid, so she and J. R.'s son, Jim, also a neophyte lawyer, researched it and found that she was right, so the matter was taken to court and J. R. won. The prime relevance of this story is that later on, after the death of my first wife, Eleanor, in 1980, I met and married this young lawyer and my best man at the wedding was none other than J. R. Miller.

As I write these words J. R. Miller has been dead for less than a month. The reader will understand why he has been so big in my life.

President Truman's Louisville Appearance

I have another story that fits in at this point, and I want to tell it because it is priceless and it needs to be preserved. Sam Stallings, a native of Bullitt County, was a highly successful lawyer in Louisville, and during one year while I was on the court was president of the Kentucky Bar Association. While Sam was president of the bar he was able to get former President Harry Truman to come to Louisville as principal speaker at the annual meeting of the bar association. The event was held in the Flag Room, on the first floor of the old Kentucky Hotel, at Fifth and Walnut in Louisville. The place was packed. I have never seen so many lawyers at anything else ever held in Kentucky. It was a festive occasion in every sense of the word.

This is an insignificant detail, and I record it only because it was a part of the occasion I remember so well. Mr. Truman was at that time a pretty old man and did not hold his water as well as most younger folks, so at least twice he had to thread his way back through the throng to get to the men's room. Each time, of course, he was accompanied by the Secret Service man assigned for his security, and each time as he passed down the aisle he was given an ovation by the crowd along the way. He was immensely popular. Whether you happen to be a Democrat or a Republican, this was a real human being, a man with guts and spirit, a real American.

One of the guests of honor at the banquet was retired U.S. Supreme Court Justice Sherman "Shay" Minton, who lived across the Ohio River at New Albany, Indiana. He and Truman were great friends. I think they had served together in the U.S. Senate, and Truman had appointed him to the Supreme Court. Minton was seated to Truman's left at the head table. Sam Stallings, chairman for the occasion, was seated to Truman's right. Anyhow, according to Sam, Truman spent so much time talking to Minton that at last, realizing it, he turned to Sam and by way of apology explained his apparent neglect of Sam, his host, as follows: "Sam," he said, "I love old Shay so much that if I loved him any more I'd just have to dick him."

The reader may doubt the veracity of this story, but I am satisfied that it is true. Not only did Sam tell it to me very shortly afterward, but he verified it to me several years later. I have told it many times to many people.

Harold Kelley and Louie Nunn

Speaking of the Truman visit to Louisville brings to mind Harold Kelley, of Ashland, another inimitable personage I would never have known had it not been for my judicial career. Harold is both a lawyer and a CPA and has made a fortune in business and accounting. He has always taken a great interest in politics. Although nominally a Democrat, he is by no means a stranger on the other side of the game (money can do that for you), and he was a devout admirer of William H. May, the man who did as much to put Bert Combs in the governor's office as anybody. When Harold learned that Mr. Truman would be in Louisville he bought a book about him and asked Bill if he could possibly get it autographed for him. So Bill managed to get it done, and returned the autographed book to Harold just before the big event at the Kentucky Hotel. Then Harold did a foolish thing, as even the shrewdest people will sometimes do. He was wearing a hat, and he put the hat, with the book under it, on the shelf of the cloakroom just off the Flag Room. You can figure the rest. When he went to get his hat after the speaking the book was gone. Somewhere today some scurvy S.O.B. has Harold's book with President Truman's signature in it.

Harold got his accounting education at the old Bowling Green (Kentucky) Business University, where he had the good fortune of befriending a classmate from Barren County named Louie Nunn. Both of them went on to law school, after which Harold became a CPA and got rich while Louie practiced law and became County Judge at Glasgow and then Governor of Kentucky. I have cherished the warm friendship of both of these outstanding men.

Shortly after Louie's inauguration in 1967 there was some kind of function at the old Frankfort Country Club that was attended by a lot of politicians, lawyers and newspaper folks. I remember meeting

Worth Bingham on that occasion. Anyway, I was standing at the bar next to Bill May, and Kelley was on his other side talking to him. When somebody else came along and momentarily diverted Harold's attention Bill turned to me, covering his mouth with the back of his hand, and whispered, "Jack, this guy's living at the governor's mansion!" Well, it was so. Louie had appointed Harold as chairman of the Public Service Commission, and Harold was temporarily lodging at the mansion with the Nunns.

I do not know what kind of a relationship existed between Bill May and Louie Nunn prior to Louie's accession to the throne (after all, as one of the most influential Democrats in the state, Bill certainly had not supported Nunn's candidacy), but it was quite cordial thereafter, and I feel pretty sure that Harold was the good fairy. Bill's highway engineering business fared quite as prosperously during the Nunn administration as it had in the Combs and Breathitt days.

A funny story Harold told me was that one time Louie attended a meeting at Bill's place and that Louie was brought over there in the back seat of an automobile with a blanket over his head so that he would not be seen. In a recent conversation with Harold I learned of the great political significance of this particular meeting between Louie and Bill May. When Nunn took office as governor in December of 1967 the state government was in very poor financial condition. The success of a new administration depended on some new source of revenue. The governor was a Republican and the legislature was heavily Democratic. Prospects of getting an increase in the state sales tax, the most promising source of new money, were quite remote — impossible, in fact, unless by some miracle enough Democrats could be won over to get it done. At that moment of history Bill May was the biggest mover and shaker in the Democratic Party. He and Kelley were warm friends. Naturally, Nunn's reaction to Harold's suggestion that they go to see Bill May was negative. But he saw the light, and this was the meeting, in the ancient little building (once a church) in Bill's back yard, that set the stage for the successful effort to jam the 2-cent sales tax effort through the legislature. Bill May, Lawrence Wetherby and Louis Cox had the political oomph to swing it. This was the keystone of what any fair-minded observer of Kentucky politics would have to concede turned out to be a constructive and successful administration — at the expense, perhaps, of a few people's political futures. The voting public sure doesn't like taxes.

Harold served as chairman of the Public Service Commission throughout the Nunn Administration and was one of Louie's most valuable and trusted advisors, but he tells me that in all of that time he was never approached by the governor, either or directly or indirectly, about any matter pending before the Commission.

William H. May

Bill May was a nephew of A. J. "Jack" May, who served for a time as a member of Congress. The Mays were a prominent family in Prestonsburg, where Bill grew up. Politics was in his blood. Early in his career he was elected as Commissioner of Agriculture, and for a time he aspired to greater office. He ran for lieutenant governor, but was defeated by Lawrence Wetherby, who later became one of his best friends and eventually worked for Bill's Brighton Engineering Company. Bill liked to tell about the time he went to see Doc Beauchamp and asked if Doc could support him in his race for lieutenant governor, but Doc said no, that Bill was his second choice. "Well, Doc, do you mind telling me who is your first choice?" asked Bill. "Any other S.O.B. that's running," said Doc.

Bill May was one of the most fabulous men I have ever had the privilege of knowing personally. He introduced himself to me one day at a U.K. football game in the fall of 1962. Later on that winter I was looking for a place to buy or rent and a friend, John Hopkins, called and asked if I would be interested in renting an old house on the Georgetown Road that Bill's company, Brighton, was renovating. Thus Bill became my landlord for the next four years, and I enjoyed his friendship for the rest of his life.

Following Bill's death several years later I sponsored a project to put up a memorial fountain in his honor at the Frankfort Country Club. Among those who attended or spoke at the little dedicatory ceremony were Bert Combs, Lawrence Wetherby, and other notable figures, including Harold Kelley, who drove down from Ashland in his

William H. May
April 1, 1974
Copyright © 1974 by the *Courier-Journal.* Reprinted with permission.

Rolls-Royce automobile and spent a nostalgic evening at our house.

Among his friends and acquaintances Bill was famous for his often-wry sense of humor. During the first session of the legislature following the election of Louie Nunn in 1967 Bill and his supporters, including Lawrence Wetherby, who was then a member of the state senate, were doing their best to help the governor get his 2-cent increase in the sales tax passed. The senator from Prestonsburg at that time was Cliff Latta, a cousin of Bill's, and according to the oft-told story, when Bill put the heat on Cliff to support the bill, quite naturally Cliff demurred – to some extent at least As everybody knows, the surest road to political oblivion for any legislator (or governor, for that matter – Louie himself has never enjoyed a howling success in politics since he prevailed in this particular instance) is to vote for a sales tax. "But Bill," Cliff is said to have protested, "that will beat me in the next election!" "Well," Bill replied, "That's a price I am willing to pay."

The Court Family

I inherited my first secretary on the court, Elizabeth Johnson, from Judge Sims. Elizabeth was a native of Morganfield and had been educated at St. Vincent Academy, a Catholic school near Waverly, a little town (famous for its unexcelled barbecue) between Henderson and Morganfield. She was very bright and smart and had been an outstanding student at St. Vincent. However, she had been deprived of a college education because her father, Truman Drury, brought her to Frankfort to work for him when he was appointed as a commissioner of the Court of Appeals. I never knew or saw Judge Drury, but I understand that he was a very large, corpulent man, and Elizabeth also was a large (but not fat) person. Somebody told me that Judge Drury never rode in an airplane, but said one time that he would go up in one if they would let him keep one foot on the ground. Though not endowed with a sylph-like figure that would attract most men, Elizabeth was happily married to an excellent man named Charlie Johnson, and she was a loyal and helpful friend to me. Incidentally, Truman Drury's brother, Lucien, a popular lawyer in Morganfield, at one time had been Speaker of the Kentucky House of Representatives. His son, George Ignatius "Snatch" Drury, one of my friends and contemporaries of early law practice, had something close to a photographic memory. My first recollection of Morganfield was the occasion of Lucien Drury's funeral in 1939.

Most of the court secretaries were great people. Personality-wise, they were pretty agreeable folks. And formidable, I might add. Usually they had worked for more than one judge over the years, and there was a good deal of camaraderie among them – as well as know-how. Montgomery's secretary had once worked in the governor's office, which gave her something of a command attitude, and whenever the secretarial corps felt it was about time for a pay raise Monty (the Chief) would show up at conference with a sheepish look on his face which told us that Opal had taken hold of his ear. Tough and resolute as Monty was in conference with a group of men, he was an absolute lamb in the hands of a woman. His sprightly wife, Tansy, could not have had a more obsequious liveried servant.

Back in those days there was a statute that required the court to be in session except during July and August. Actually, no one paid any attention to it, and we had three terms, a long fall term beginning in September, three weeks off for Christmas, two weeks off for Easter, and then several weeks off for the summer. All in all, I think we were in session for 36 weeks of the year. Anyway, one of the secretaries had a regular second job during the summer in a downtown Frankfort office, and when the court eventually decided to have each of the secretaries be on duty for one week in the summer this dear old soul took great umbrage at such an unwarranted incursion of her livelihood(!).

Astor Hogg

The 1956 federal elections had been an Eisenhower landslide, sweeping out every Democrat up and down the line, including my great and good friend Senator Earle Clements. Another casualty was Astor Hogg, a member of the Court of Appeals from Harlan, who was defeated by Bob Bird. The court had then hired Astor to do administrative work, such as handling motions. When I came onto the court in 1959 my library adjoined Astor's office, with a door between, so in due course we got to know each other pretty well. A native of Roxana, in Letcher County, Astor had been a circuit judge before his election to the Court of Appeals. He was a good judge and an excellent, likable, jovial man. We all loved him. He liked to take a drink (or more – though his good wife Gertrude generally managed to keep him on a tight leash), and was an inveterate cigarette smoker. One day while I was working in my library (where I spent most of my time) I smelled smoke, and then saw it seeping under the door from Astor's office. I jumped up and threw the door open, and there was Astor sitting at his desk beating his hands at a pile of papers afire on the desk in front of him. It seems that as he was bending over his work with a cigarette hanging out of his mouth a hot ash had fallen onto the papers and set them on fire.

One of Astor's experiences while he was judge of the Harlan

Circuit Court provides a vignette of how things must have been in that part of Kentucky in the old days. One day while he was presiding at the trial of a murder case and the defendant was on the witness stand a kinsman of the man who was alleged to have been murdered jumped up with a pistol in his hand and shot the defendant dead. On being asked what was his reaction to this dramatic event, Astor would say, "Why hell, I dropped under the bench as fast as I could!"

Astor Hogg
Ca. 1960
State Photo

My funniest memory of Astor involved a young lady we had working for somebody on the court, and who was said to have something of a cozy relationship with one of the judges. She was pretty good-looking, and didn't mind using a little come-on. At the time, I was living in an apartment off Murray Street and usually walked to and from the Capitol. One morning as I was going up the stairway toward the clerk's office, just as I turned the corner I heard this sweet little unctuous voice say, "You sure do smell good this morning!" And there she was, standing in the hallway next to a blushing, squirming Astor Hogg, who probably had used an extra-fragrant after-shave lotion that day. Believe me, if looks could have killed when I showed up at this embarrassing moment, the one this girl shot at me would have been fatal.

Jim Milliken and Brady Stewart

Life on the court was not always dull. One time before I came along Jim Milliken, who lived at Cold Spring, in northern Kentucky, and customarily came to Frankfort on Tuesday, which was the regular day for full-court conference, happened to come in on Monday, a day early. As he opened the door to his office somebody hastily disappeared through the door to an adjoining chamber, and there sitting

Brady M. Stewart
Ca. 1960
State Photo

naked on the couch was a comely young female employee of the clerk's office. In the shock and confusion of this extraordinary event the good judge dropped his briefcase and ran excitedly down the hall to report it to his fellow judges. The lady lost her job, of course, but they never were able to pin anything on the male culprit. The prime suspect was a rather handsome young administrative officer of the court who had keys to all the offices and was familiar with Jim's custom of not coming in on Mondays.

One of my favorite judges on the court was Brady Stewart, from Paducah. Brady was born at Monkey's Eyebrow, in Ballard County near the confluence of the Ohio and Mississippi Rivers (great duck and goose-hunting country). He was County Judge of McCracken County for some time before being elected in 1950 to succeed Gus Thomas, the longest-serving judge of the old Court of Appeals. I remember that election, because, although I did not live in that district, I knew and liked his opponent, Ira Smith, the circuit judge in Hopkinsville, and hoped that he would win. But Brady was an old Earle Clements man, and in those days that was strong medicine, as it was later on, when I enjoyed the same beneficent fortune.

For having been a country boy, Brady had attained a high degree of cultivation. He was an inveterate play-goer and never missed going to New York every year to see the newest shows on Broadway. Though probably not the intellectual peer of a Cullen or Lukowsky (or, later, a Leibson), he was sound and solid as a rock, full of common sense and absolutely dependable. Once he came to a decision he was there to stay. Milliken, on the other hand, kind and sweet as he was, always anxious to help somebody (or everybody), had as hard a time sticking with a tough or controversial opinion as a tenderfoot trying to stay aboard a bucking bronco. You will recall, for example, his having vacillated back and forth in the broad-form deed battle. I'll never forget the time we had a hard-fought struggle over a liquor case from Richmond. When the I-75 highway was built, the strip between it and the city (and the Eastern Kentucky University campus) very quickly filled in with various businesses. The city was wet and the county was dry, and it so happened that this connecting roadway between I-75 and Lancaster Avenue was just outside the city limit. So, when this enclave was annexed by the city it precipitated a lawsuit as to whether the new part of the city automatically became "wet" like the rest of the town. Otherwise, the local option statutes required a wet-dry election for the entire magisterial district in which newly-annexed strip was located. The remaining (and major) part of this district was, of course, rural in character, and as I recall had voted "dry" some years before, so it was not likely that the tail could wag the dog this time.

James B. Milliken
Ca. 1968
State Photo

We had a vigorous oral argument on the case and an equally vigorous battle in conference. It was decided on a 4 to 3 vote, to the effect that the annexation did not make the disputed area "wet." Milliken and I were two of the three on the losing side. It was our feeling that it would not make good sense for a large, rural part of the county to have the say on whether this small part of the city should be wet or dry. Anyway, in due course the case came up on rehearing and again we had a hot and lengthy bout in conference. Finally, my colleague Ed Hill, who was sitting next to me at the conference table, and who had voted with the majority, said something to the effect, "Jack, you've convinced me. I'm going to change my vote." This, of course, would turn the case around, so I thought I had won out. But wait – our old cohort Milliken, sitting down at one end of the table puffing on his pipe with a big frown on his forehead, cut his eye over at Bev Waddill, who had written the opinion for the court, and said, "Bev, you had a hard time writing that opinion, didn't you?" "Yes, sir, I did," said Bev. (Actually, Bev wouldn't have given a damn one way or the other.) Jim drew another puff or two on his pipe and then said, "Well, I'm going to stick with it!" Here endeth the lesson.

Earl Osborne

It was a sad day for those of us on the court when Brady Stewart got beat for reelection in 1966. As so often happens in political life, in his 15 years living away from home he had lost touch with a generation of voters and apparently suffered also from the wounds of the 100 percent tax assessment case, as Squire Williams later did in 1968. Brady was beaten by Judge Earl Osborne, of Benton, who had become circuit judge by defeating Judge Henry H. Lovett. There was a good deal of local bitterness against Earl arising from these two contests by reason of the kind of campaigns he is said to have conducted. Up until that time I think it had not been customary for judicial candidates in western Kentucky to sling mud at each other, especially at a sitting judge, but Earl was a pretty blunt character, not given to pulling any punches, and I don't doubt that he was something less than delicate in those two races. It simply was not in his nature. Whenever an obstacle appeared in Earl's way it was his instinct to bow his neck and run over it, not around it.

Earl came onto our court with a chip on his shoulder, and for the next eight years things were never the same as before. He knew that the other judges liked and had been for Brady in the election, and quite naturally he resented it. Hence from time to time we endured sparks of belligerence on his part. And he was a large, physically powerful man, so we had to bear it in silence. Ordinarily, that is. Once we had a case in which he rather strongly disagreed with the rest of the court and had to settle for writing a dissenting opinion. Some time later the case came up on a petition for rehearing and the chief justice (I don't remember off-hand who it was at the time) assigned it to Earl. This may seem odd, but often as a tacit gesture of courtesy a case on rehearing would be assigned to a judge who had dissented from the opinion.

Earl T. Osborne
Ca. 1968
State Photo

Anyway, we had another rather spirited argument in conference over the merits of the petition for rehearing in this case, and still the majority of the court held to its opinion, which had been written by Ed Hill. Evidently Earl got into something of a huff and decided that he would just hold the damn file in his office and not send it over to the Clerk's office until he got good and ready. Well, after two or three weeks had gone by Ed began to wonder what had become of his case, and went over to Earl's office to see about it. As Ed told it to me afterward, Earl's response was that he just didn't know how long it would be before he was through with it – maybe never. Now Ed was not a milk-toasty fellow either, and they almost came to blows right there in Earl's office. It ended with Ed going back to his office pretty well steamed. Some time later, after things had cooled off and Earl had regurgitated the file, Ed told me that for several days he had been carrying a pistol to the office, because he "wasn't going to let that big son-of-a-bitch hit me."

Earl Osborne is dead and gone, and what I have said thus far about him is not intended to demean him. Certainly it does not reflect the whole picture. Each of us has his own personal faults and idiosyncrasies. He had an excellent mind and was well able to hold his own in a logical discussion. In time we became reasonably good friends. From long observation I have come to believe that what people want the most from other people is respect; I respected him, and I think he respected me. Incidentally, for a time Earl's son Tom, who now practices law in Paducah, served as his law clerk and was well liked by all of the court family.

One of Earl's chief supporters in his race against Brady was Boyce Clayton, a lawyer in Benton. Evidently Boyce thought that Earl owed him something, or had promised him something, but didn't do whatever Boyce was expecting, and when Earl's time for reelection came up eight years later Boyce ran against him and won. So, during the last eight years of my time on the court we had Boyce, for better or for worse. We always tried to see that he had a good law clerk – one of whom, Larry Cleveland, is today a successful lawyer in Frankfort.

Pleas Jones

Of all the judges with whom I served over the period of 23 years I had the greatest personal affection for Pleas Jones, of Williamsburg. Pleas had come up the hard way – worked in the coal mines, taught school, served in the Army during WWII, and went to U.K. Law School under the G.I. Bill of Rights. He told me that he and his sweet wife Marie had courted for four years before he was making enough money for them to get married. However, his sunny disposition and genial personality made him a natural for elective office, and before long he had been circuit court clerk and then county judge of Whitley County and was the circuit judge of that district before coming to our court following the death of Judge Homer Neikirk, of Somerset. At that time we had a judicial council which met in our office once a month, and I had come to know and appreciate him through his membership as the circuit judge representative in that group. The circumstances under which he was appointed and then elected to our court are worth the telling:

Early in 1973 Homer suffered a severe heart attack, and needed open heart surgery, which at that time they did not do at the U.K. Hospital or anywhere else closer than Cleveland, Ohio, or Duke University in North Carolina. One day shortly after Homer had come home from the hospital in Lexington his wife, Opal, called me on the telephone and asked if I minded coming over to their house, here in Frankfort, which of course I was glad to do. They told me that arrangements had been made for Homer to undergo open heart surgery at Duke, but they were afraid that he would not be physically able to make the trip by automobile. Wendell Ford was our Governor at the time, and they knew that he and I were friends, so they asked me if I

Pleas Jones with Boyce Clayton in the background.
Ca. 1974
State Photo

would mind seeing if Wendell might be willing to have Homer flown to Durham in the state plane. (Homer being a hard-nosed Republican and Wendell a Democrat, the Neikirks probably felt a little shy about approaching him directly.) Well, the governor responded without hesitation, and it was no sooner said than done. The Neikirks were flown to Durham in the governor's state plane.

Sadly, Homer died from complications following the operation, and the governor and I flew to Somerset for his funeral. During the trip Wendell asked what I thought about whom he might appoint to fill the vacancy. He had a good friend and supporter in Somerset who would have liked to have the appointment, but he was a Democrat and the appellate judicial district was so heavily Republican by that time that it would have been an exercise in futility except for the honor of the thing. Wendell was aware of Pleas' popularity, and I was enthusiastically for him. Wendell knew also that he would be running for the U.S. Senate later on and that it would not hurt for him to have the good will of the Republicans in that district. In due course he appointed Pleas.

At this point one of those incredible developments came to pass. Pleas, of course, had to run in the next election for the remainder of Homer's unexpired term, and because it was too late for a primary the nomination or nominations were to be made by the party committees, consisting of the county chairmen as I recall (this was before nonpartisan judicial elections were established by the 1975 Judicial Amendment). At this time Charlie Coy, of Richmond, was the state chairman of the Republican party. He took exception to Pleas' having committed the unthinkable offense of accepting the appointment from a Democrat, and exercised his influence to block his nomination by the committee, with the result that Circuit Judge Bob Helton, of London, was chosen as the Republican nominee. The only recourse for Pleas under these circumstances was to run as an independent candidate or not run at all, a choice that did not offer much hope of success. Pleas chose to run, odds or no odds, and By George he won!

When I read the good news in the *Courier-Journal* the morning after the election I went to my office, got a sheet of my official stationery and wrote one word, "Hallelujah!" Then I put that message on Pleas' desk where he would see it as soon as he came in from Williamsburg and went to his office. Needless to say, he got a big bang out of it, and I think he treasured that little note for the rest of his life.

Pleas had a lot of wit and was a great story-teller. He also enjoyed having a drink or two (on occasion). Once while I was chief justice I was invited to speak at a bar association dinner at a nice little country club down in the Greensburg area, which was in Pleas' district, so he too attended the meeting, and was called on to make some remarks before I spoke. Naturally, he told some stories and cracked a few jokes, and by the time all the talking was over most of us had imbibed as much or more as the law would allow. But the funny thing that happened was that after I had finished speaking, for some reason or another Pleas got up and spoke again, and not only did he speak again, but he told some of the same stories over again!

I guess I didn't know that Pleas was going to be there at that dinner, because we came down from Frankfort in our separate automobiles. It was a two or three-hour drive back to Frankfort, at night, and Pleas followed me all the way. I distinctly remember being on pins and needles during the entire trip for fear that one or both of us would be apprehended by the hounds of the law, but the kind Lord was with us, and we made it without incident.

One of Pleas' best stories needs to be preserved in print for posterity, so as best as I can I will undertake to retell it here. Whether it is truth or fiction I do not know, but he told it as if it really was so. It seems that one day while he was county judge he met a friend named Leander on the street. Leander was employed at a little country garage several miles from town. Pleas saw that his friend appeared to be unusually downcast, so after they had exchanged greetings he asked Leander what was the matter. "Lord, Pleas, you just ain't gonna believe it," said Leander. "Well what happened?" Pleas asked, to which Leander replied that yesterday morning when he had gone to work he had forgotten to take his eyeglasses, which he normally had to wear while doing mechanical work, so he decided to go back home to get them. "Well," said Leander, "when I got to the house I saw this car out front that I didn't recognize, but I didn't pay no attention, I just thought some other lady was visiting my wife, so I went on in and walked back to the kitchen, because that's where you would usually find her, but there wasn't nobody there. That's strange, I thought, maybe she's sick or something – so I goes to the bedroom and the door was closed. Naturally I opened it, and Pleas, thar on the bed, nekkid, was my wife, a-layin' thar with a man I ain't never see'd before!" "My God, man, what did you do?" Pleas exclaimed. "Well that's the thing, Pleas, there wasn't nothin' I *could* do!" said Leander. "Hell, man, what do you mean, nothing you could do?" "Well, Pleas, don't you know, they both laid right thar and lied out of it!"

Pleas retired at the end of 1978 without having run for reelection. Ten years later, at Marie's request, I spoke at his funeral in Williamsburg. I also wrote the memorial resolution presented to the court on October 17, 1988. It appears in the prefatory pages of 761 S.W.2d. When Pleas died I called our old colleague Earl Osborne, in western Kentucky, and reported it to him. I quoted his response in my remarks at the funeral, and again in the memorial resolution, because

I think it was the definitive epitaph: "Well, anybody that didn't know Pleas really missed something." That says it right. And despite our occasional differences I am glad, too, that I knew Earl Osborne.

Osso Stanley

In my days on the court we had some great people, including Judge Osso Stanley, one of the all-time greats of the court. I think he had started as a court reporter over in Bardstown and was one of the last of the old lawyers who rose to the bar through "reading" law – that is, without having been law-college trained. Whatever may have been his legal training, or lack of it, he was about as well-read a lawyer as I have ever seen, thoroughly versed in the fundamentals and, as I have already indicated, a positively superb writer. Unquestionably he was proud of his literary prowess, as he had a right to be. An apocryphal story the old hands on the court used to tell about him was that sometimes when he had written an opinion and then the court had turned it down and decided the case the other way he would just rewrite the last few lines and change the holding (called the "cracker") from "affirmed" to "reversed," or vice versa. He did have a wondrously facile pen.

Osso W. Stanley
Portrait in the State Capitol
Courtesy of Sally D. Flynn

In those days, when an opinion had passed muster at the full-court conference on Tuesday the commissioner or judge who had handled the case and written the opinion would send the whole record, with the opinion, over to our administrative office. On the following Friday the record (a bundle of papers tied up with red tape) would be placed on the judges' bench in the courtroom, in front of the seat occupied by the author of the opinion, except that because the commissioners did not sit at the bench, their opinions were placed randomly, so that, for example, if I had two opinions of my own to announce, not only would those two records be at my place, but there might be one or two or more that came from commissioners. Then in open court each of the seven judges would announce the decisions in the cases in front of him and hand the records down to the clerk of the court, or a deputy. Now the reason for this lengthy rigmarole in this otherwise humdrum piece of literature is that one time Judge Stanley had a hard time getting an opinion approved by the court. Week after week he kept bringing it back to conference, but for some reason or other it got badly stymied, and finally no more was heard of it, and the rumor leaked around that Stanley had got so dad-gummed tired of seeing that old record in his office that he just bundled it up and sent it on as if it had been decided and settled – with the result, of course, that it went down on Friday with the rest of the opinions. I can't vouch for this, but it could easily have happened.

Another thing that could and did happen from time to time was that after an opinion had been passed in conference its author might polish it up, change a few words, or even materially alter it before sending it to the administrative office for handing down on Friday. I remember, for example, that one time I had written a dissenting opinion and for some altruistic reason made the mistake of showing it to the judge who had prepared the majority opinion, whereupon, as I later discovered, he proceeded to doctor up his majority opinion so as to put my dissent in a bad light without giving me an opportunity to see what he had to say. As often said, there is many a slip between the cup and the lip.

At the risk of unduly boring the reader I want to mention one or two more of my colleagues for whom I had great respect and affection.

Sam Steinfeld and Bernard Davis

Sam Steinfeld, who held the seat from Jefferson County for eight years, was one of the most agreeable and courteous people on the court. His wife Flora was equally gracious. At this writing they are both

Sam Steinfeld
Ca. 1968
State Photo

living. Sam's only problem was that he was a Republican, but at least he was a good Republican. There was only one time that this unfortunate circumstance created any embarrassment on the court. After the death of Judge Stanley we had a vacancy for a commissioner, and Morris Montgomery was hot to give the job to Bernard Davis, of Shelbyville, which of course was in his district. The reader will recall my having said that this district, which included Pulaski County, was heavily Republican. That may have been something of an overstatement, because after all, Monty was a Democrat and he had been elected. Nevertheless, the Republican party in that district was robust and healthy, and Monty lived in dread of what might lie ahead at his own next election. Shelby County lay at the northern end of the district, and it was Democrat country. Obviously it was to his advantage to have as many friends as possible in that county, as well as to eliminate whatever competition for his own office that might be lurking in that neck of the woods. Monty was a good politician. He believed in having strong friends in strong places. Davis, moreover, was a brilliant, outstanding lawyer, and had graduated with high honors from Washington and Lee, Monty's alma mater. So it came to pass that we agreed to the appointment, and I will have to say that this man was a real whirlwind. He worked night and day, did some lusty drinking and partying on the side, and turned out about twice as much work as anybody else on the court. When Monty and Tansy got killed in that terrible automobile accident later on Bernard decided to run for Monty's seat on the court against Homer Neikirk, who had been appointed by the Republican Governor Louie Nunn. He lost. By this time, politically, the color of that district had become distinctly

Republican. Monty's apprehensions in that respect proved to have been well founded.

Davis was still on the court as one of its commissioners, which did not suit Homer Neikirk at all. As I have said already, Homer was a hardnosed Republican, and this man had run against him, so Homer was resolved to get rid of him. We all liked Bernard, and everybody appreciated his great value to the court, so for a long time Homer could not get three other votes to oust him. This is where Sam comes in. He did not want to have Bernard fired either, but one day he came in to conference sort of hanging his head and said that he was going to have to give in. Nobody asked him why, but it was clear that he had been turned by party pressure. So it was that we lost Davis – on a 4 to 3 vote.

Bev Waddill and Bob Lukowsky

Another favorite of mine on the court was Beverly B. Waddill, of Madisonville, whose appointment as a commissioner had, I think, been sponsored by Brady Stewart. Bev was a tall, fine specimen of a man, who had played football at the University of Kentucky. He was unfailingly courteous and kind and was a sound, dependable judge. Bev's brother, Cliff Waddill, was the circuit judge at Madisonville and was known for running a tight, no-nonsense court. Cliff also was a tall and courtly man who carried himself like a gentleman. My wife and I enjoyed the good company of Bev and Martha Waddill on many an occasion before he retired to Madisonville.

Bev Waddill
Ca. 1968
State Photo

Cullen, Clay, Lukowsky, Scott Reed, and Bernard Davis were the truly brilliant men on the court during my time. Anyone who makes a point of reading their opinions will have no difficulty in recognizing the truth of that

Robert O. Lukowsky
Ca. 1980
State Photo

assessment. Lukowsky probably had the finest mind of the whole crowd, but unfortunately, he had a short fuse, and did not suffer fools gladly, with the result that a good many lawyers in northern Kentucky who had smarted under his rule as circuit judge succeeded in blocking his effort to get an appointment to the federal bench. In this, Bob was his own worst enemy. He simply could not resist using the needle. For the last few years of my time on the court my eventual successor, Bill Gant, was a member of the Court of Appeals, and from time to time his opinions would come under review by our court. Somehow Bob took a special delight in picking Gant's opinions apart, and after a time Bill got the idea that for some unknown reason I was the culprit, which cost me what had theretofore been a cordial relationship with Bill. Bev Waddill, Sam Steinfeld, Pleas Jones, Jim Milliken, and Squire Williams probably were the most congenial and good-natured. Gentlemen all!

Before signing off on Lukowsky I must tell you about a notable gaffe he made during one of our committee reviews of the Kentucky Penal Code as it was being drafted. As I have said, the principal drafter (actually the father of the work) was none other than Bob Lawson, who is remembered today as an outstanding dean of the U.K. College of Law, a greatly respected scholar and teacher. As it happened, Lukowsky had a question about something in the part of the draft we were reviewing that day, and in the course of the colloquy it developed that he and Lawson did not see eye to eye. After an exchange or two the steam began to come out of Big Luke's ears and he ended the discussion with the remark that "after all, you are only the scrivener anyway." This did not set too well with the alleged "scrivener," but of course he was too polite to respond in kind.

Martin Turner

One more and I am finished. It was once customary for the governor's staff of house-servants to be drawn from the state penitentiary, and at the end of his term they would be pardoned. One of these, Martin Turner, a gentleman of color, was working for the court as its janitor when I came to Frankfort. I think he had been pardoned by Governor Willis. Apparently he went to the pen for killing his wife, but there never was anything warlike about him that I could see, and he was held in high esteem by all the folks around the court. He was reputed to be the best "varmint" cook in town, though I never had an occasion to feast on any of his vaunted victuals. Unquestionably he was a very likable character. One time while he was still with us I bought an undersized pool table and got Martin to come out to the house and help me set it up. When we got through Martin said, "Let's hit a few." "Okay," said I, "You break 'em." So Martin picked up a cue-stick and proceeded to run the table in rapid order. I was shocked. "Where did you ever get to shoot pool like that?" I asked. He gave me a sly grin, turning his head a little sideways, and said, "Oh I used to shoot a little pool around these towns like Georgetown and Lawrenceburg and such, but after a while they all got to know me and wouldn't nobody take me on any more." In that sweet land of bye and bye, God bless old Martin!

The Law Clerks

When I first became a judge I had no use for the idea of having a law clerk, and for some years I worked without one. I still think a judge ought to do his own work and will do a better job if he does. However, it finally dawned on me that by not having a law clerk I was depriving some young law school graduate of an opportunity to spend a year with the court, which I know is a valuable experience for the young lawyer. So, over the years I had a number of clerks, splendid young men and women, and I learned how stupid I was not to realize what dear friendships come to a judge through these years with his clerks.

Two of my old clerks, Julia Tackett and Gary Payne, have been judges of the Fayette District and then Circuit Court. Julia has since become a judge of the Court of Appeals, and Gary is still on the circuit bench in Lexington. Mike Caudill is County Attorney of Warren County. Pat Moloney and Kevin Henry are prominent attorneys in Lexington. Chris Gorman, of Frankfort, whose gracious, popular mother, Polly, was an invaluable member of the governor's staff back in the time of Combs and Breathitt, has served a term as Attorney General of Kentucky as well as a county commissioner of Jefferson County. Others are successful practicing attorneys in various places in Kentucky, as are many who worked for other members of the court. Bill Graves, for example, who clerked for Jim Milliken, is at this writing (2003) a member of the Supreme Court of Kentucky. Richard Thomas, of Bowling Green, is a top executive and chief counsel with Ashland Oil.

I have always remembered one day when a humble young Italian-American boy named Jim Tardio came up to my office in the state capitol and asked if I could give him a job as a law clerk. As a kindly fate would have it, I had recently lost my clerk – I don't recall which one it was – and I was captivated by this young man's honest face and respectful manner, so I hired him on the spot. He came from New York state – Syracuse, I think – and after his time with me he landed a job with a law firm in Greenville, Kentucky, and is a successful practitioner there today. From New York to Muhlenberg County, Kentucky, my friends, in more ways than one is quite a jump, but I know without asking that the same fine qualities that endeared him to me have not been lost on the people of that western Kentucky community.

Among the other former clerks for whom I have special affection are Raymond Smith, of Louisville, whose father, Russell Smith, a great tax lawyer, was one of my lifelong best friends, Grant Helman, of Louisville, who has distinguished himself for his long years of outstanding service on the Character and Fitness Committee of the bar association, John Baughman, of Frankfort, whose father was my friend and physician (on the night my first wife, Eleanor, died suddenly at home Doc came over to our house with his pajamas still on), and John Hay, also of Frankfort, a great grandson of the famous Col. E. H. Taylor, Jr. I met John under somewhat unusual circumstances. One night about the time he graduated from law school I was in the bar at the old Frankfort Country Club and several young fellows were sitting together at a table. I knew one of them, and went over to shake hands with him. As I came to the table one of these boys, and only one, stood up. That was John Hay. This gesture of old-fashioned courtesy impressed the hell out of me, and later on, after I learned that he was going to be a lawyer, I persuaded John to put in a year as my law clerk. Today he is one of my best friends. He has his hands full trying to manage his old family home place, Scotland Farm, and does not have time to practice law any more, but he is every inch the gentleman I took him to be that night at the old country club years ago. There aren't many like him.

Gary Payne, the court's first African-American law clerk, and Judge Palmore. December 14, 1979
State Photo by Steve Mitchell

To the best of my knowledge and belief, our court had never in its history had an African-American law clerk, and when I became Chief Justice I was resolved to bring one aboard. So I called Bob Lawson over at the UK law school and asked him to help. (Incidentally, I know this isn't quite relevant, but it gives me an opportunity to say what I think about Bob Lawson. The law and lawyers of Kentucky have been blessed to have such a man. He has been much more than a great teacher and a great dean of the law school. He has given of himself for the good of the profession willingly and freely – and modestly. I doubt that historians will be able to do him half the justice he deserves.) Bob referred me to one of his recent graduates, Gary Payne, a native of Paducah who had served a hitch in the U.S. Marine Corps and had been a good student at the law school. Gary was just about to sign up with the IRS, but somehow I was lucky enough to change his mind (or help him to change it), and he signed on with us. To make a long story short (for which I have no great talent), he did a superb job and then went on to practice law in Lexington, where he was elected first as a district judge and then as a circuit judge. There is a good deal of the old confederacy in Lexington (more, I believe, than there was in the 1860's), and I guarantee that it was not easy for Gary to win election to the local judiciary, but he did it. During his time as a district judge the lawyers of the community came to know and respect him for his dignity, honesty, and ability, so that when it came time to run for the higher office of circuit judge the path was easier than it had been when he first ran for district judge. People like Gary taught me how wrong I had been in not wanting a law clerk in the first place.

I had one law clerk who was almost like a son. His name was John Cowgill, and he was from Lexington. John was the child of a broken home (in the sense that his parents were divorced), and I think he needed the affection my wife and I had for him. He spent a good deal of time at our house, helped me train my dogs, and became a real companion. After completing his clerkship he went off to the army for a year, as I recall, and when he was released from his military duty at Fort Knox the first place he stopped was at our house. Shortly after he started to practice law in Lexington he suffered an aneurism, or something of that nature, in his brain, and the doctors were not able to save him. This just about killed us. My grief at his death was as great as it was when I lost my own son several years later. Again, as I said about Martin Turner, may God bless the memory of that wonderful boy. I would have been proud to be his father.

There are a number of others, of course, that I could mention. I cared a great deal for all of them, and I expect that some of them will carry me out when I go.

Other Notables and Compatriots

I could go on and on about the people in and around the court while I was there. Our clerks, Doris Owens and John Scott, my administrative assistants Howard "Bud" Trent and Bob McBeath, my last secretary, Eunice Mayes, our great and brilliant little court chronicler Nancy Lancaster, Bev Waddill's kind and wonderful secretary Bertie Cheshire, Clarence Williams, who succeeded Martin Turner and later retired after working for the state for 39 years, bar association major domo and now Clerk of the U.S. District Court in Lexington, Les Whitmer, our old state librarian the distinguished General Field Harris (formerly second in command of the U.S. Marine Corps), the bar association trips and cruises, the judicial conferences in such places as Alaska, Jackson Hole, Williamsburg, Flagstaff, Baton Rouge and Biloxi, the wonderful people I met and got to know – like Justice Bill Brennan, Howell Heflin, Chief Justice of Alabama and then a United States Senator from that state, Judges Roger Traynor of California, Wally Schaeffer of Illinois, Vince McKusick of Maine, Joe Henry of Tennessee, Oscar Knutson of Minnesota, Ted Souris of Michigan (a companion at the New York seminar in 1961 and one of my dearest friends until his death in 2002) – and so on, but even life must come to and end, so this is about as good a time and place as any to go ashore while the ship is still in port.

Index

A

B

C

D

K

L

M

N

O

P

ABOUT THE AUTHOR

John S. Palmore was born in the Panama Canal Zone on August 6, 1917. He graduated from Bowling Green (Kentucky) High School in 1934, attended Western Kentucky University and the University of Louisville School of Law, was admitted to the Kentucky bar in 1938, and practiced law in Henderson, Kentucky from 1939 until 1959, except for two periods of military service during World War II and the Korean Conflict. He served as City Prosecuting Attorney and later as City Attorney for the city of Henderson from 1953 until 1955 and as Commonwealth's Attorney for the 5th Judicial District of Kentucky from 1955 until 1959, when he was elected to the old Court of Appeals of Kentucky to fill the unexpired term of the late Judge Porter Sims. He served twice as Chief Justice of that court before it was renamed in 1975 as the Supreme Court of Kentucky. He retired from the latter court at the end of his third term of office after having served as Chief Justice from 1977 to 1982. For the next 10 years he practiced law in Frankfort, Henderson, and Lexington, and retired in 1992. Judge Palmore is the author of *Palmore's Instructions to Juries (Civil)* and numerous articles and papers.